BUILD YOUR OWN DATABASE

Péter Jacsó

AND

F. W. Lancaster

AMERICAN LIBRARY ASSOCIATION
Chicago and London
1999

Project editor: Joan A. Grygel

Text design by Dianne M. Rooney

Composition by the dotted i in Berkeley Book using QuarkXPress 3.32

Printed on 50-pound Arbor Offset, a pH-neutral stock, and bound in 10-point coated cover stock by Edwards Brothers

The paper used in this publication meets the minimum requirements of American National Standard for Information Sciences—Permanence of Paper for Printed Library Materials, ANSI Z39.48-1992. ∞

Library of Congress Cataloging-in-Publication Data

Jacsó, Péter.
    Build your own database / by Péter Jacsó and F. W. Lancaster.
      p.   cm.
    Includes index.
    ISBN 0-8389-0750-4
    1. Database design. I. Lancaster, F. Wilfrid (Frederick Wilfrid), 1933- .
  II. Title.
    QA76.9.D26J33   1999
    005.74—dc21   98-41983

Printed in the United States of America.

03 02 01 00 99   5 4 3 2 1

Contents

Figures

Preface

Modern technology has made it possible for more and more organizations to create electronic databases and to distribute these (in CD-ROM or other forms) or to make them accessible via the Internet. We produced this book in the hope that it would help people to produce databases of better value and quality, especially if they have had little previous experience in database construction.

Librarians have found themselves increasingly involved in database production and distribution activities, and it was this audience that was uppermost in our minds when we began to put the text together. For librarians and for others who are in a similar situation (in corporate, academic, or other settings), the book offers guidance on content of the database and on software aspects of implementation. The book may also be useful as an introductory text in courses dealing with database design and implementation.

We have attempted to make our text practical and user-oriented. We define database quality not in theoretical terms but solely in terms of the potential utility of the database to its intended users.

Drawing upon our experiences in the field of information retrieval, which extend back almost forty years, we emphasize basic principles and approaches rather than in-depth and comprehensive evaluations of particular products. Some of the most popular text management programs were selected for illustrations. All of these run under Windows; some of them also run under Mac OS. (The capable Library Master program is not included because the Windows version is not available at this time. Similarly, a widely popular Windows program, AskSAM, was not included as it was in the process of being upgraded at the time of this writing. It is a particularly appropriate program for creating databases for unstructured, full-text documents.) It is clear that the trend is moving away from DOS toward the Windows platform. Some of the programs discussed in the book evolved from bibliography formatting software, such as ProCite, Reference Manager, and EndNote. Others, such as DB/TextWorks and Micro-CDS/ISIS, were designed from the ground up as textual information retrieval programs with particularly strong indexing and search capabilities. There has been a convergence to endow the bibliography formatting software with more powerful indexing and search capabilities and the textual information retrieval programs with improved output facilities.

Many other programs in addition to those mentioned in this book can be used to build textual databases. The focus here is on programs that are well-supported, well-documented, and widely used by librarians and other information professionals in libraries and information centers. For example, no mention is made of high-end programs such as Oracle or Sybase because they are very expensive and require computer specialists for efficient deployment; these are typically used in large corporate information systems. New programs for the target audience of this book may appear on the market, as did the excellent Biblioscape program from CGI, Inc., in the summer of 1998 at an introductory price of $99.

The criteria discussed in this book can be used to gauge and evaluate the capabilities of other programs that librarians may consider in microcomputer-based library automation projects. These criteria are intended for the computer-literate librarians who have used some online or CD-ROM databases and are interested in building their own databases. The book is not a manual on how to use these programs but a guide to the considerations and options when creating a database in a library or information center.

Acknowledgments

I am grateful to Wilf Lancaster whose idea it was to write this book and who was able to interest ALA in its publication.

I learned the most about microcomputer software for library automation in general, and database development in particular, through designing and implementing various types of databases. They ranged from directories to abstracting/indexing and full-text databases (enhanced with searchable page-images). Working with other people was enriching in these endeavors.

I am grateful to John Eyre, retired senior lecturer of North London University, whose excellent special course on library automation showed me a model for teaching in general, and this subject in particular, and who motivated me to become an educator in the 1970s. I have been fortunate to work with Professor Emeritus Jerry Lundeen whose database reviews, articles, and textbook (coauthored with professor Carol Tenopir) helped me in developing a systematic approach to teaching database design and implementation. For a decade I have been lucky to have had Larry Osborne, a fellow faculty member, former interim dean, and program chair, working next door at the University of Hawaii. He was not only capable but also willing to bail me out when I got stuck with hardware or software problems.

Throughout the decade of teaching database development courses I have had students who excelled in hashing out ideas, trying out alternatives, and arguing intelligently and competently. I think with great pleasure of students in my database classes, especially Jenifer Winter, Janet Hesson, Marcia Kemble, Benjamin Cheng, Joely May, Rae Shiraki, Rich Gazan, Pam Cahn, and Richmond Aea. I also learned a lot from many of my former colleagues, especially Varga Sanyi and Huba Zoli, and from systems developers at the Hungarian National Library (Berke Zsuzsa, Szilvássy Judit, and Szücs Peti). I thank Dr. Luciana Marulli-Koenig for having given me the opportunity to develop several databases and for critiquing many of them in the process.

I learned the most from Szücs András, currently working as a computer specialist for the World Intellectual Property Organization. He has been not only a very competent programmer with an always upbeat and cooperative attitude but also a superb partner in every aspect of developing databases and automation projects for well over a decade. I thank Joan A. Grygel, the editor of the manuscript, for her many clarifications and suggestions.

As always, my utmost thanks go to my wife, Tiszai Judit, who has not only been supportive in all these endeavors in more ways than one but has actively participated in the design and implementation processes of many of the projects.

—Péter Jacsó

PART I

Content and Organization of the Database

1

What Is a Database?

The term *database,* as used in this book, refers to any collection of records in electronic form. Here *electronic form* means "capable of being read and otherwise manipulated by computer." Frequently the records in a database represent something else, usually a physical object such as a book or other publication, a piece of art, an archaeological artifact, or even a person (as in employee records or records of patients in a health care situation). In other cases, however, the records are complete in themselves. For example, they may be compilations of various kinds of statistics, or they may comprise the complete text of some set of items—such as correspondence, technical reports, or articles from newspapers and magazines.

Database Creators

The building of databases was once complex and expensive—an undertaking restricted to government agencies or large enterprises. In the last several years, however, this situation has changed considerably because of the dramatic decline in the cost of computing, the proliferation of personal computers, the emergence of CD-ROM, and most significantly, the explosive growth of the Internet and the World Wide Web.

Today, many organizations, some of them quite small, find themselves in the position of creating databases for their own internal use or for the use of others. In some cases, the database is designed to be sold (for example, as a CD-ROM) or made network-accessible on a fee basis. Builders of databases include manufacturers that develop databases of correspondence, contract files, and engineering drawings; libraries that develop databases of local government records, local history, and community resources; museums and art galleries and their databases of some or all of the pieces in their collections; hospitals with their patient record databases; and research groups.

Database Quality

It is now relatively easy to produce a database, but this, in itself, does not guarantee that the database will be useful. To be useful, a database must be built in such a way that information can be derived from it effectively and economically. To a very great extent, this retrievability depends on what information is included in the records, what form the information takes, and how the records are structured.

Based on the results of research, experimentation, and practical experience over a period of more than thirty years, a considerable body of knowledge now exists to help us build databases that will be as useful as possible. Our objective in this book is to explain what makes a database "good" and, thus, to provide guidance to those faced with the task of creating a database.

Scope of the Book

The main emphasis of the book is the building of databases by a single organization, whether for internal use alone or for outside sale or access. However, a broader perspective is also introduced in places, namely the building of databases by some geographic or political entity. Questions such as "Should a small country build a national database, and if so, what should it include?" are dealt with where they seem appropriate. The difference between the organization-level perspective and the broader one applies only to the justification for the database and to its content. Quality factors remain the same.

In considering databases and their implementation, a distinction can be made among the three aspects of hardware, software, and dataware. *Dataware* refers to the contents of the databases (what is included and how it is presented and organized), while *software* refers to the capabilities provided for exploiting the dataware (user interface, searching capabilities, output capabilities, and so on). Hardware aspects are outside the scope of the present book, but major software and dataware requirements are both dealt with.

Database Types

As defined previously, many different types of databases exist. One possible way of categorizing them is as follows:

> bibliographic databases
>
> full-text databases
>
> image databases
>
> databases referring to other physical objects
>   (that is, other than text or images)
>
> numeric and statistical databases
>
> descriptive databases
>
> directories and other "reference sources"

The term *bibliographic database* usually refers to a database containing records that represent various types of publications. Each record *describes* a publication—gives the title, names of authors, publisher, date of publication, perhaps physical characteristics (for example, number of pages), and terms indicating what the publication is about. The most obvious examples of bibliographic databases are the catalogs of books in a library or databases referring to articles appearing in scholarly periodicals or popular magazines. Note that, as commonly used, the term *bibliographic* refers only to databases that contain records representing publications and not to databases that contain the actual text of the publications. In fact, the scope of the term can legitimately be extended to include databases that describe any type of collection consisting primarily of text (whether published or not). Thus, a database containing records that refer to a company's correspondence files (but not containing the text of the correspondence) could be considered "bibliographic," as could one referring to the contents of the company's contract files or, in a different context, one referring to the records of a local government.

A full-text database is similar to a bibliographic database in that it deals with items in the form of text. However, as its name implies, a full-text database contains the complete text of the items it includes and not just records representing them. Examples include databases containing the full text of newspaper or magazine articles, laws, a company's technical reports, the messages in an Internet discussion group, or the correspondence of some organization.

An image database, as the term is used in this book, is similar to a bibliographic database in that it contains records describing things. In this case, however, the items described are in pictorial rather than text form—paintings in an art gallery, photographs, or more specialized items such as radiographic images. Image databases present problems somewhat different from those encountered in compiling bibliographic databases. For example, the item may not have a definitive title, and it may be important to describe not just what is represented but how it is represented—for example, where an object appears in a photograph or painting, its color, and its texture.

Databases can also deal with physical objects other than those in text or picture form, for example, catalogs of exhibits in a museum or of flora of a particular region. Again, this type of database may present requirements not present in the other types—for example, a piece of pottery may need to be described by shape, dimensions, color, and date.

Other databases consist primarily of numerical values. These include statistics of various types, such as records of sales or scientific data such as data on the thermophysical properties of materials.

Descriptive databases are compendia of various kinds, such as descriptions of the resources of a particular geographic region, the programs offered by a university or college, or the capabilities of a company. Many of the home pages existing on the Internet can be considered brief descriptive databases. Clearly, descriptive databases will consist primarily of text (although numerical values and images may be included), so they are related to the category designated as *full text*. However, the latter term is most frequently used to refer to the electronic equivalents of printed publications. The more general term *text databases* could be used to include all that consist primarily of narrative text.

The final category of database is one that is the electronic equivalent of some type of reference book, such as a directory of organizations or individuals or a dictionary. Clearly, databases of this type can combine elements from the other types. For example, an encyclopedia would include images as well as text. Moreover, it is likely to exploit the full capabilities of the medium, including motion and sound, and to allow for some interaction with the user.

It should be obvious that these categories are not completely watertight, but the classification is adequate for present purposes. The characteristics dealt with in the rest of this book apply to databases in general, although, where appropriate, characteristics peculiar to a particular type of database will be highlighted.

The terminology relating to compilations of electronic records is far from standardized. For example, the term *databank* is sometimes used, primarily in Europe, to refer to collections of numerical data. The term *data warehouse* is now used increasingly in industry to refer to a database of corporate intelligence, especially when this resource can be used for data mining or data exploration. For our purposes, the term *database* will be used to represent collections of electronic records of any type used in any application.

2

Database Content

When considering the creation of a new database, or perhaps in justifying the continuation of one already in existence, matters relating to content will be the major concern. Some important criteria governing justification for the existence of a database include:

domain of coverage
accessibility of content
predictability of coverage
continuity of coverage
currency of coverage
critical mass

These are all related in some way to the contents of a database.

In looking more closely at these factors, it is necessary to make a distinction between databases designed for the internal use of an organization and those intended to generate a profit by charging for access or selling in CD-ROM form. In the latter case, obviously, market-related factors will be paramount. That is, the estimated cost of building and maintaining the database must be balanced against the probable size of the market and the price that customers might be willing to pay. In the case of an internal database, the cost of building and maintaining it has to be balanced against its probable value (usefulness) to the organization.

Domain of Coverage

The major justification for creating a database is the fact that the material to be included is not covered or not well covered elsewhere. It makes little sense to duplicate resources that already exist in a suitable form.

Take the case of a manufacturing company that also performs some research in support of its operations. A database that provides access to publications dealing with the company's interests would undoubtedly be of great value. However, this literature may already be well covered by existing databases produced by government agencies or other organizations, so it is pointless to duplicate this coverage. On the other hand, the company's own internal resources—its technical reports, contract files, and correspondence—will not be accessible unless they are adequately indexed within a company database. These are also the resources that are likely to be of greatest value to the organization.

Nevertheless, even though the published literature (for example, published reports and articles in periodicals) may be well covered in commercially available databases, an organization may be justified in building its own specialized database by downloading relevant records from the external databases and even, perhaps, combining the external records with those created to cover the organization's internal resources. This would be particularly true if the organization (for example, a company) has highly specialized interests or it has interests so diverse that they would only be covered by a large number of existing databases. A single comprehensive database, tailored to the organization's particular interests, may be justified by factors of convenience and by the likelihood that important information will more easily be found when the need for it arises.

Records downloaded from external databases may well include index terms describing the subject matter of the items covered. Nevertheless, although subject indexing tends to be costly, the reindexing of these records could conceivably be justified to make them compatible with records for internal resources. Reindexing might also be justified when the terms used in the imported records are not specific enough to reflect the organization's specialized interests. (See chapters 3, 6, and 7 for a discussion of various aspects of indexing factors.)

Of course, the records appearing in external databases are normally protected by copyright. The downloading of these records will require agreements with and payments to the database producers.

So far we have considered the database issue from the viewpoint of the single organization, but the situation can have a more global perspective. Smaller countries, particularly those that are less developed, face the issue of whether to build a "national" database and, if so, what to include in it. In fact, the national perspective is not too much different from the perspective of the single organization. To make the situation more concrete, let us assume some mythical country. We will call it "Treeland."

Clearly, it would make no sense for an institution in Treeland to create a database that would largely duplicate one of the international databases that already exist. Therefore, it is obvious that the highest priority should be given to the coverage of publications generated in the country itself since these are not likely to be well covered by the major databases produced in the United States, the United Kingdom, and elsewhere. National coverage could be extended to regional coverage (that is, including the production of neighboring countries) where the subject matter of the database is of national importance and the broader geographic or language scope is needed to complement the coverage of the international databases.

Fully justified also are databases that include publications about the country, for example, a database on Treeland trade that includes both national publications and publications on Treeland trade that are produced elsewhere. The justification here is one of convenience. Even though the non-Treeland items about Treeland may be well covered in the international databases, it is convenient to bring them together with the locally produced items, particularly if they are dispersed over several of the international databases.

The fact that a database of reasonable size *could* be constructed on the basis of Treeland publications alone does not, in itself, justify its creation. For example, it would rarely be justified to build a database that is essentially a subset of an existing Treeland database—such as an air pollution database if a general "environmental problems" database exists or a database of national theses in a single subject area if a complete thesis database exists. Such duplication encourages the needless proliferation of databases and, thus, the increasing fragmentation of knowledge.

Under most circumstances, it would not be justifiable for a Treeland institution to create a truly international database—one that attempts to include all the world's literature on some topic. However, exceptions to this general rule could exist. For example, it would be justified to build a comprehensive database (drawing from all the world's literature) on some specialized subject area that is particularly important to Treeland when a specialized database on this subject does not already exist elsewhere. Perhaps the most obvious example is a database on a particular crop or group of crops that are especially important to the national agricultural economy. Such examples exist in other countries—for example, a coffee database in Costa Rica, a sugar database in Cuba, and a banana database in Panama. A similar situation might apply in the area of public health; that is, a comprehensive international database might be justified if it dealt with a disease or group of diseases that are particularly prevalent in Treeland.

Accessibility of Content

The criterion "domain of coverage" applies most obviously to bibliographic databases and to those devoted to statistical or numerical data. For other types, different criteria may be more appropriate. For example, databases that present images and descriptions of artifacts—objects in a museum, paintings in an art gallery, or all artifacts of a particular type (masks or traditional costumes)—are easy to justify on the grounds that they collect images of artifacts that may be widely dispersed geographically or that they make available to students and scholars images of collections that they may not easily be able to visit for themselves. Improving the accessibility of artifacts and works of art, through photography, is a major justification for the existence of image databases, especially when the collections involved are unique to a particular country or region.

Content accessibility has dimensions beyond that of geography. For example, a full-text database may be justified by the fact that the ability to search it by computer greatly facilitates intellectual access to the contents of the text itself. Thus, the full text of a newspaper going back to its beginnings, on CD-ROM, can be much more valuable than having the newspaper bound as print on paper, not only for convenience of handling and for preservation purposes but also because of content accessibility when the text can be searched for various word combinations.

Predictability of Coverage

The criterion "predictability of coverage" relates primarily to the production of databases for distribution (for example, through sales) rather than for the exclusive internal use of an institution. To be useful to others, the coverage of a database must be fully predictable. The subject matter dealt with must be *precisely* defined. A database that covers a heterogeneous group of subjects that are loosely connected is of little value because potential users will not know what is included and what is not.

Within the domain dealt with (subject area or type of material), coverage should be complete, or as complete as one can make it. A database that claims "selective" coverage of some topic or type of material is of very limited value because potential users are unlikely to know what the criteria for selection have been. In the case of a database that indexes articles in periodicals, the database producer must make clear which periodical titles are covered and must be consistent in indexing all issues. If certain contents (for example, letters to the editor or obituaries) are excluded, this also must be made clear.

In a similar way, a database that claims to include the full text of a journal, or group of journals, for a particular period, should include all issues and all articles for this period. Users will have little confidence in a database if they find unpredictable and inexplicable gaps in its coverage. Predictability is an important element in building confidence among users and potential users.

Continuity of Coverage

No institution should produce a database that requires updating unless it is willing and able to make a commitment, especially a financial commitment, to keep it up-to-date. A database that covers only a few years—of a particular journal or of publications in a particular subject area—and is not supplemented or otherwise updated is of little use to anyone. While an institution may well have good reasons for discontinuing a particular database (for example, because it has been supplanted by another that is more comprehensive or broader in scope), it will lose credibility if it discontinues the database for reasons that are not obvious to subscribers or other users.

Currency of Coverage

Some databases will never need to be updated (such as one that reproduces the works of a deceased artist), while others, existing mostly for archival or historical purposes, may need to be updated very infrequently. On the other hand, databases that are intended primarily for current awareness purposes must be updated often if they are to retain their value. Clearly, a database of ongoing research must include research projects that are still in progress, rather than completed, and preferably should get projects represented at about the time they are beginning. A database containing information on conferences and other meetings must include listings for these events long before they actually take place, and a bibliographic database devoted to a particular subject area must be updated often, preferably no less frequently than quarterly if in CD-ROM form and more frequently if accessible online. Updating should be predictable, occurring on a regular schedule. "Irregular" updating is unsatisfactory from the consumer's point of view.

Critical Mass

Probably the most controversial of the content-related criteria is that of critical mass, referring to the fact that a database must be large enough to be of interest and value to a significant number of potential users. "Large enough" is not a precise concept; it cannot be quantified exactly. However, it would be difficult to justify a bibliographic database in CD-ROM form on a subject so specialized that only a hundred or so items are published on the topic each year; it might not be economical to update such a database on even an annual basis.

Catalogs of libraries present another case. For a library of major national importance, it may be worthwhile to publish the catalog on CD-ROM for further distribution. In the case of libraries of lesser importance, however, the catalog of one library is not likely to be worth further distribution. Catalogs representing the holdings of several libraries will be much more valuable. However, to be useful, a catalog of multiple libraries must have some underlying logic. That is, it should include libraries that are logically connected in some way—all dealing with the same subject matter or all libraries in a particular city or region.

A database containing the full text of a journal or newspaper can be justified if the publication is one of special importance, particularly if the temporal coverage is complete (that is, if it goes back to the beginning of the publication), because a database of this kind may have archival or historical significance. However, a database that covers several newspapers or one that includes the text of several journals (if they are in the same subject area) is likely to be much more valuable than one devoted to a single publication.

A database containing the full text of papers presented at several conferences may be worthwhile, provided that the compilation is a logical one (all the conference papers of a particular body for a period of years or all the conference papers falling in some broad subject area). In contrast, a database containing the text of papers given at one or two isolated conferences is unlikely to have a great deal of value.

Similar criteria apply to other types of databases: Images of artifacts in several museums are likely to be of more value than those restricted to one museum (unless it is of unusual size and importance); likewise for art galleries. A database devoted to the work of one artist may be justifiable, but one devoted to the work of several artists may well be more valuable, provided that the artists are logically connected in some way (such as all being from the same region or all sharing a particular style or form).

Critical mass is not just a matter of useful size. In the long run, it relates also to matters of fragmentation and of the economics of access. This applies most particularly to databases distributed on CD-ROM. The cost of producing a large database on CD-ROM may not be much more than the cost of producing a small one. Since institutional budgets are limited, the proliferation of small databases tends to reduce accessibility as well as the size of the potential market for CD-ROM products. For example, an institution that may be willing and able to purchase a CD-ROM illustrating the work of, say, five artists may be unwilling or unable to purchase five such disks, each dealing with a single artist. The fragmentation factor, which affects databases accessible through the Internet as well as those on CD-ROM, is also significant. In general, it is more efficient and economical to search one more-comprehensive database than to search several smaller ones that are in closely related subject areas, especially when each database may employ completely different approaches to indexing and may require the use of quite different search strategies and search terms.

3

Quality and Usability Factors

Quality is not something that is abstract or theoretical when applied to databases; it is a very practical issue. A database can be considered of high quality if it is useful to the community it is designed to serve; it can be considered of low quality if it is not useful to that community.

One important factor affecting the usefulness of a database has already been dealt with, namely its content. However, in itself, the content of a database is not enough to make it useful. To be useful, the database must be constructed in such a way that users can retrieve useful information from it without having to expend an excessive amount of effort. Thus, the major criterion of quality, after content, has to do with the *retrievability* of database records.

Retrievability Factors

Figure 3-1 lists the major factors that govern what is retrieved when a search is performed in some database. Note that the factors fall into two major categories: those relating to the database itself and those relating to how the database is searched. A detailed discussion of search strategies is outside the scope of this book, although it is touched upon later in chapter 8. Nevertheless, it should be clear that the search approach that can be used in a particular database, to a very large extent, is governed by the characteristics of the database. To take an obvious example, one cannot search on dates (for example, of publications) if dates do not appear in any records. The database characteristics affecting retrievability are dealt with in the following sections. In this discussion, the primary concerns

Figure 3-1 Major Factors Affecting the Retrievability of Records

Characteristics of the database itself
Number of access points
Consistency of terminology
Specificity of access points

Characteristics of the search approach
Completeness of the approach
Specificity of the approach
Capabilities of the searching software

are with the representation of subject matter within the databases and the searching of databases by subject rather than by names (for example, of authors) or other elements. The handling of names is not necessarily a trivial problem, but subject representation and searching offer much greater complexity and thus deserve the emphasis given them here.

Number of Access Points

A record is retrieved when some "element" used to query the database appears in the record. The search element will usually be a word or phrase, but it could be something else, such as a numerical value or some type of code. In rare cases, it may be some form of image that matches an image appearing in the database. Usually, too, elements are combined in some way rather than being used alone. Thus a search on the term "dogs" will retrieve only records in which this word (that is, string of characters) occurs; "dogs OR cats" should retrieve only records in which either word (or both) occurs; and "dogs AND alaska" will retrieve only records in which both words occur. The words used in these examples are access points, so-called because they make the records accessible (retrievable). Clearly, the more access points that a record has, the more likely it is to be retrieved.

The relationship between number of access points and retrievability is well illustrated in figure 3-2. Here, an indexer has tried to represent what an article in *Newsweek* (April 21, 1997) is about at three different levels. The article deals primarily with science and how research in science and the interpretation of research results may be influenced by political and social concerns and social fashions. This central topic has been covered by the indexer through the four terms chosen in Level 1 indexing.

Figure 3-2   Three Levels of Access to Subjects in "The Science Wars"

Level 1	Level 2	Level 3
Science	Science	Science
Politics	Politics	Politics
Social influences	Social influences	Social influences
Fashions	Fashions	Fashions
	Constructivism	Constructivism
	Women's studies	Women's studies
	Literary criticism	Literary criticism
	Expansion of the universe	Expansion of the universe
	Cosmology	Cosmology
	Animal behavior	Animal behavior
	Heritability	Heritability
		Hubble constant
		Baboons
		Ornamentation
		Abortion
		Cancer

To illustrate this central subject, the author of the article introduces various examples. In Level 2, the indexer tries to represent the more important of these additional topics as well as the central subject matter by introducing further terms, and this process is carried further in Level 3.

What effect do these various levels of indexing have on the retrievability of a record for this article included within a database—say one covering the articles in popular magazines? It is obvious that a Level 1 record can be retrieved only when a searcher uses one of the four access points or a combination of these four—such as "science AND politics." However, this article may also be of interest to someone searching for information on a slightly different topic. For example, the article has some relevance to the influence of women's studies on the interpretation of the results of research in science. The record should be easily retrievable with Level 2 and Level 3 indexing since the terms "science" and "women's studies" are both present. Conceivably, it might also be retrieved with the Level 1 indexing, but this would require much greater ingenuity and perseverance on the part of the searcher. For example, the searcher would have to recognize that "women's studies" could be considered a "social influence" vis-a-vis science. More importantly, the search could not be limited to the specific topic of interest—everything on social influences on science would be retrieved (possibly a great number of items in the case of a large database), and most of these would not be of any relevance or interest.

Level 3 indexing would allow this article to be retrieved by other searchers of the database who might find it to be of relevance to different interests. For example, someone may want to find all articles in which views on abortion may have influenced the interpretation of the results of research in science. The article could be retrieved with the Level 3 indexing but not at Levels 1 or 2—at least not easily and not without retrieving a great deal of irrelevant material.

This article does not deal in a very major way with the relationship between the abortion issue and the interpretation of research results. Nevertheless, it may be worth retrieving, especially if this is a topic on which very little has been written or on which little has been written in the popular press. Moreover, even if the reference to this subject is rather slight, the article may give the searcher a lead to further information. For example, the article mentions two relevant articles appearing in medical journals and also gives the name and institutional affiliation of an academic researcher whose work has been at the center of this particular issue.

Finding the Optimum Level of Indexing

One could conclude that everything in the database should be indexed as completely as possible—at Level 3 in the example or even beyond it. This is not necessarily so—for two reasons. First, when human intellectual effort is used, indexing thoroughly will be more time consuming, and thus more expensive, than indexing at a more superficial level. (Some alternatives to human indexing are discussed toward the end of this chapter.) Second, the more completely an item is indexed, the more likely it is to be retrieved in cases in which it will be judged irrelevant. Returning to the example of figure 3-2, the Level 3 indexing (in particular) covers topics that are dealt with in only a very marginal way in the article. True, the article does refer to the Hubble constant (a measure of the rate at which the universe is expanding), but it really does not give much information on the subject. Someone doing a serious search on this subject (or on baboon behavior, cancer, literary criticism, or other topics dealt with tangentially) may well say that this article deals so little with the topic as to be useless. If very many items like this are retrieved, the searcher may not put much trust in the database.

The Level 3 indexing also creates other problems: The more terms used to index an item, the more likely it is that *completely* irrelevant items will be retrieved because the terms will suggest relationships that are completely false as far as this article is concerned. For example, the article could be retrieved in a search for information on the use of baboons in cancer research (because "baboons" and "cancer" are both access points at Level 3), but it has no relevance whatsoever to this topic. While false relationships can occur at any level of indexing ("fashions in politics," "fashions in literary criticism," and so on), they will obviously be more prevalent when many terms are used than when few are.

What this suggests is that there is likely to be some "optimum" level of representation of an item within a database. Except for some unusual situations, the optimum is not precisely quantifiable: We will not be able to say, for example, that ten terms is "right" but eleven is too many and nine is too few. On the other hand, based on practical experience, we may be able to conclude that indexing at around ten terms per item (on the average) seems to give better results than indexing at five or at twenty terms on the average.

The best level of indexing in any situation will depend on the characteristics of the items represented in the database and how the database is used. If the users of a particular database always need comprehensive searches—they can't afford to miss anything—detailed indexing will be needed even though, for reasons mentioned earlier, this may often produce a search of low relevance. Although comprehensive search needs do exist, perhaps in certain health care or customer support (help desk) situations, this is fairly unusual. More commonly, a database user will be looking for those items that give the most information on some topic rather than every possible reference to the subject.

The characteristics of the items included in the database will also exert a great influence on the number of access points required. The more complex and multifaceted the items covered, the more thoroughly they will need indexing. Within an engineering company, for instance, the company's contract files may be worth indexing in very great detail, with terms representing all the materials used, operating conditions (such as temperatures and pressures), dimensions of products, and so on. The detail of indexing is warranted not just because of the size and complexity of the files but because of the great importance of these resources to the company. The cost of the detailed indexing is more than justified if it prevents the company from investing in the redesign of a component it had designed once before or if it prevents the company from repeating a costly design or installation error.

Different categories of materials may be indexed at different levels, even within the same database, because of differences in their complexity or value to the organization. Thus, in the database of an industrial organization, the company's own technical reports should probably be indexed in greater detail than reports acquired from outside sources, and articles of interest to the company, drawn from technical journals, might be indexed with even fewer terms.

Notable Exceptions

While the guidelines on number and type of access points will apply in the great majority of cases, more unusual situations may exist in which different criteria would apply. In discussing the example illustrated in figure 3-2, it was pointed out that topics dealt with in only a very marginal way should probably not be indexed. Nevertheless, there are exceptions to this. For example, the *Newsweek* article referred to includes the names of several universities whose research programs have figured, one way or another, in the controversy discussed. One could imagine some organization building a database dealing with the relative influence of different universities in science research. In this case, names of the universities would be very important access points. There are other occasions where something mentioned in a publication should be included as an access point even when the mention is very slight. An obvious example relates to the newness of the topic—a new drug, treatment, alloy, or whatever. Picking these up in the indexing is justified by the fact that little or nothing has been written on these topics before.

Text Search

Human indexing tends to be labor-intensive and expensive, so there is much interest in finding alternative approaches to making items accessible through some database. In the case of bibliographic databases, at least, two alternatives are possible: text searching and automatic indexing. Automatic indexing is discussed later in the chapter. The text search situation is dealt with here.

Text search implies that the database contains text stored in electronic form and that the text is searchable. That is, a searcher can use the search programs to look for text in which a particular word or word combination occurs. The text stored can be as complete as the entire item—an entire article from a newspaper or periodical, an entire technical report, a piece of correspondence, or whatever—or it can be less than the complete text—an extract of some kind, a summary (abstract), or perhaps merely the title of the item.

Today, of course, most text printed on paper existed first in electronic form. This, coupled with the fact that electronic storage has become so cheap, has led to the creation of many large databases of complete text. Almost all searching within the Internet involves the searching of complete or partial text.

It is certainly convenient to have complete text in electronic form so that it can be viewed on a screen or printed out on demand. Nevertheless, being able to search complete text is not always better than being able to search something less complete, such as an extract or abstract. When searching a database for text relating to a particular topic (information retrieval), the length of the text stored affects retrievability in much the same way that different levels of indexing do, as illustrated in figure 3-2. This can be demonstrated by considering the short article appearing in figure 3-3. The complete text of the example can be stored in

Figure 3-3   Brief Article Illustrating Various Possible Levels of Text Search

The Academic Boycott of South Africa:
Symbolic Gesture or Effective Agent of Change?

F. W. Lancaster
University of Illinois at Urbana–Champaign
and
Lorraine Haricombe
Northern Illinois University

From the early 1960's until very recently, scholars in South Africa were subjected to various forms of boycott within the international academic community. The academic boycott, strongly supported by the African National Congress and various agencies of the United Nations, was part of a much broader sanctions campaign—including political, economic, cultural and sports elements—designed to express condemnation of the policy of apartheid and to force change in the racial policies of the South African government. The academic boycott was intended to "isolate" scholars in South Africa by depriving them of the formal and informal sources of information needed to further their research and of the conduits through which they could bring their own work to the attention of the international community.

Manifestations and Levels of the Boycott

At least eight manifestations of this boycott can be recognized:

1. Scholars refusing to travel to South Africa or to invite South Africans abroad;
2. Publishers, journals, and the like refusing to publish South African manuscripts;
3. Scholars abroad refusing to collaborate with South African scholars;
4. Publishers abroad refusing to provide access to information (for example, books or computer software);
5. International conferences barring South Africans;
6. Institutions abroad denying South Africans academic access;
7. Institutions abroad refusing to recognize South African degrees;
8. Scholars abroad refusing to act as external examiners for theses presented at South African universities.

Elements of such a boycott can exist at national, institutional, or personal levels. At the national level, for example, some countries—including Japan, India, Finland, and the Soviet Union—routinely denied visas to South Africans. At the institutional level, scholarly bodies prevented South Africans from attending their conferences, rejected manuscripts submitted for publication, or otherwise put obstacles in the way of scholarly discourse with South Africans. Trinity College, Dublin, provides an extreme example: it forbad its faculty to collaborate with South Africans, threatening those who disobeyed with censure or dismissal.

Views on the Boycott

The ethical and other issues surrounding the academic boycott deeply divided the academic community, both within and outside South Africa. Boycott proponents argued that academics should not be treated as an elite detached from the political and social environment in which it functions, especially since some of the South African universities seemed to be tools of the Nationalist government.

Opponents of the boycott argued that ideas and knowledge should be treated differently than tangible commodities, that obstacles to information access could actually hurt the victims of apartheid (for example, retard medical research and, ultimately, reduce the quality of health care), and that an academic boycott (in contrast to economic, trade or political boycott) would not even be noticed by the South African government. Change is much more likely to occur by providing information than by withholding it.

A compromise position, advocated by some, was that of "selective boycott" or "selective support"—organizations in South Africa should be boycotted if they practiced apartheid and supported if they opposed it. This approach was also severely criticized both because of the practical problems of implementation and because it implicitly endorsed the idea that political views are valid determinants of who should attend scholarly meetings, whose work should be published, and so on.

A Book Boycott

A particularly controversial element in the academic boycott of South Africa was the "book boycott." Books, journals and other scholarly materials were not included in the trade boycott enforced by the United States under the terms of the Comprehensive Anti-Apartheid Act of 1986, but some countries, such as Denmark, applied an absolute embargo. Elsewhere, individual publishers, booksellers or other vendors were free to adopt their own policies.

Both the Association of American Publishers and the Association of American University Presses opposed an embargo on scholarly materials. Nevertheless, several major U.S. publishers imposed their own boycott. One was University Microfilms International, which cut off the supply of dissertations to South Africa, causing one South African librarian to point out that getting materials from the Soviet Union had become easier than getting them from the United States.

A large and vocal element within the American Library Association (ALA) favored an absolute boycott, and some public libraries (and their parent entities) refused to do business with any publisher, bookseller, or other vendor that continued to trade with South Africa. A resolution introduced at an ALA conference in 1987 to oppose the book boycott on the grounds that it violated First Amendment rights was labeled "racist" and decisively defeated. Individual libraries, in the United States and elsewhere, refused to supply photocopies or other materials to libraries in South Africa. In some cases, requests were returned with anti-apartheid slogans scribbled across them.

Impact of the Boycott

During the year 1990–1991, we surveyed a random sample of faculty in all disciplines in twenty-one South African universities to determine what effect the boycott had on their scholarly activities. (There are actually twenty-two such institutions, excluding those in the homelands, but we accidentally omitted one.) The survey used both questionnaires and interviews.

Of the 900 questionnaires mailed (300 in the sciences, 300 in the humanities, 300 in the social sciences), 513 (57%) were completed. Forty-two faculty members were subsequently interviewed in their faculty offices in South Africa.

A second questionnaire was mailed to twenty-eight research libraries in South Africa to determine the effects of the boycott on their acquisitions and services. Twenty-three responded. Eight of the librarians were subsequently interviewed in South Africa.

Continued

Figure 3-3 *Continued*

Since survey results are extensive, we can only give highlights here. (For more detail, see, Haricombe and Lancaster, *Out in the Cold: Academic Boycotts and the Isolation of South Africa.* Arlington, Va.: Information Resources Press, 1995.)

About 57% of the respondents had experienced some boycott effects. A higher percentage of scholars in the humanities and arts reported effects than in the other disciplines, but scholars in the sciences were more likely than the others to consider the effects severe. Faculty at the English universities were more likely to report effects than those at the Afrikaans universities. Faculty at the "ethnic" (mostly Black) universities were least likely to report effects. Refusal of scholars to visit South Africa and difficulty in obtaining information resources were the boycott effects reported most frequently (155 scholars affected by the former and 153 by the latter). Of the 513 respondents to the questionnaire, 76 (15%) reported denial of attendance at conferences abroad, 48 (9%) reported problems in collaborating with scholars abroad, and 31 (6%) reported manuscript rejection by foreign publishers.

Comments on the questionnaires, together with the results of the interviews, lead us to the following general conclusions:

1. The numerical results of the survey are likely to underestimate the extent of the boycott effects because some scholars applied "self boycott" (e.g., not applying to conferences abroad, not submitting to certain journals).
2. The academic boycott was more of an irritation than a true obstacle to scholarly progress.
3. In most cases, scholars and libraries were able to circumvent the boycott one way or another—e.g., by using "third parties" in less antagonistic countries—although with delays and at greater expense.
4. The academic boycott actually had some effects that could be considered beneficial. Lacking convenient access to foreign textbooks, some faculty members wrote their own, more appropriate to the South African situation; some departments moved from the study of Dutch literature to the study of the domestic literature.
5. The boycott had intangible, psychological effects that are difficult to assess. Many scholars felt left out, isolated, unjustly discriminated against. Suspicions were created—for example, that a submission was really rejected for political reasons, not the reasons claimed, or that the high incidence of inactive research materials, such as biological agents and antibodies, received by South African institutions was not a mere coincidence. Barriers to the free exchange of information with foreign scholars seem not to have improved collaboration at the local level. Indeed, scholars frequently felt that the isolation brought more local acrimony than local harmony.

Writing in 1986 (*Journal of Applied Philosophy* 3, 59–72), W. H. Shaw pointed out that a boycott can have actual effects or it can be merely "symbolic" (for example, serve to assuage the conscience of individuals who are otherwise passive). That most of the scholars in our study judged the boycott to be an irritant or inconvenience, rather than a significant barrier to scholarly progress, suggests that it proved more a symbolic gesture than an effective agent of change.

SOURCE: Reprinted from the newsletter *Perspectives on the Professions* 15, no. 1 (fall 1995): 3–5.

a database in a form in which it can be searched. Alternatively, one might store in searchable form only part of the article (perhaps the section beginning *Manifestations* . . .), that is, an extract. The opposite extreme from the complete searchable text is to make only the words in the title searchable. Finally, one could prepare a summary (abstract) and make it the searchable element rather than the complete text.

In short, while the entire text is stored in electronic form for display or printout purposes, the text available for searching could be

the title only

an abstract

an extract

the full text

Analyzing the Example

The title is obviously the briefest record, and the full text is the longest. The extract and abstract fall in between; these could be roughly the same length or one could be a little longer than the other.

For a searcher looking for information on the academic boycott of South Africa, the central subject of this article, the title alone would be enough to cause it to be retrieved. However, the text can be considered relevant to other topics, such as book boycotts, publishing boycotts, or conference boycotts. If the complete text is searchable, the article could be retrieved for any of these topics. Unfortunately, it might also be retrieved in searches for topics merely mentioned in passing in the text. People looking for information on "dismissal of faculty members," "study of Dutch literature," or "psychological effects of isolation" would be likely to retrieve this article based on full text (because the probable search words are all present) but unlikely to judge it useful: Although these topics are mentioned in the text, the references to them are very slight. More importantly, searching the full text could cause the article to be retrieved in completely irrelevant cases: publishing in Finland ("publish," and variants of it, and "Finland" both occur in this text), expense of health care, librarians in sports, and many other instances.

The extract designated (section headed *Manifestations* . . .) is midway between the title and the full text in both length and retrieval effects. It goes beyond the title in allowing the article to be retrieved in searches for which it may be considered useful (publishing boycotts, conference boycotts, and so on) and avoids some of the false retrievals that would occur with the complete text—but not all of them (the Finland and publishing examples and others would still apply).

The text search situation, then, is similar to the human indexing situation illustrated in figure 3-2: The brief record allows the item to be retrieved on only the central subject dealt with (social and political influences on science, academic boycotts of South Africa) but not in searches for the less central subject matter. At the same time, the brief record avoids much irrelevancy in searching. The most complete record, on the other hand, makes the item most retrievable but can lead to a lot of irrelevancy. A record of intermediate length falls between these two extremes and might be considered closer to the optimum for many purposes.

Titles, of course, can be good or bad indicators of content. The South African article has a title that indicates fairly clearly what it is about, whereas the title of the *Newsweek* article, "The Science Wars," gives no clear indication of its subject matter.

It must also be recognized that the South African article is a very short one. In a more typical situation (an article of 8 to 10 pages or a technical report of, say, 100 pages) a much greater difference will exist between the briefest record and the most complete one. It is not difficult to imagine the number of false relationships (and thus the amount of irrelevancy) that could occur in a retrieval system based on report texts, each around 100 pages in length.

The extract mentioned in connection with the South African article was chosen because it seems to be the section of text that best indicates what the entire article is about, although it is by no means ideal. The other possible representation mentioned earlier—an abstract—could conceivably be better for retrieval purposes.

The term *abstract* is usually applied to a summary of some text item prepared by a human (automatic methods will be referred to later in the chapter). For example, the following might be written as an abstract of the South Africa article:

> From the early 1960s until very recently, faculty at South African universities were subjected to various elements of academic boycott as a form of protest against apartheid. The boycott affected publishing (South African manuscripts were rejected by international journals), conference attendance (South Africans were refused access to international conferences), and scholarly research in general (for example, scholars refused to travel to South Africa, to receive South Africans, or to collaborate on research projects). A "book boycott" imposed by some publishers and booksellers impeded South African libraries and scholars in acquiring certain scholarly materials. A study of the impact of the boycott, involving use of questionnaires and interviews, concluded that it was more a symbolic gesture and a source of frustration than a serious obstacle to scholarly progress.

The abstract seems better than the extract in indicating what the article is about. It covers the more important topics (but, of course, not everything mentioned) and avoids many of the spurious relationships (but not all of them). However, an abstract must be prepared by someone skilled in summarization, so it is more expensive to produce than an extract.

To summarize the discussion on number of access points, the retrievability of a record in a database is determined primarily by its length (for example, number of index terms or amount of text). The larger the records in the database, the more accessible they will be (that is, the greater the probability that they will be retrieved). Unfortunately, while large records improve the chance that a database user will find items that are relevant, they also improve the chance that irrelevant items will be retrieved.

The discussion on number of access points has assumed that the database is bibliographic, as defined earlier. Indeed, the text search capability is associated almost exclusively with bibliographic databases. Nevertheless, the principles remain the same whatever the type of database: The retrievability of a photograph is determined by the detail in which its content is described, the retrievability of statistical data by the detail of the indexing of the statistics, and so on. *By the detail* here means number of index terms or length of textual description.

Consistency of Terminology

All of the elements included in a database record should be presented consistently and unambiguously. In some cases this is essential. For example, 4/9/1998 as the date of a piece of correspondence is ambiguous unless we know that day always precedes month.

For other data elements, the consistency may not be so essential. However, consistency will usually be desirable to save the time of database users and to avoid their frustration or annoyance. If names are not given consistently, a user may not retrieve all records associated with the name or may do so only after several searches. Is De Solla Price retrieved through *d, s,* or *p*? Is Sparck Jones retrieved through *s* or *p*? How do you deal with a corporate name such as E. I. Dupont de Nemours & Co.?

Librarians have developed rather precise and elaborate rules as to what form of name to use, and many of the large database producers either follow these or adopt rules of their own. While elaborate rules are important for very large databases, they are not so necessary in other applications. Nevertheless, consistency is still desirable. For example, it does not matter too much whether De Solla Price is entered under *p, d,* or even *s,* but the form chosen should be the same throughout the database.

For many purposes, consistency can be achieved by adopting the form of name used by some larger database producer and sticking to this form throughout.

Subject Indexing

The discussion on number of access points dealt primarily with access points that, in some sense, represent the subject or the characteristics of an object, and it is in using access points of this kind that consistency is especially important. To take a somewhat trivial example, it would be easier to find all database records on mice if "mice" appears in all of them, rather than "mice" in some and "mouse" in others. And it would not help the searcher for information on the undesirable consequences of taking a particular medication if some records are indexed under "side effects," some under "adverse effects," some under "adverse reactions," and others under "toxic reactions."

Subject indexing refers to the description of subject matter (usually the subject dealt with in some publication) by the use of terms selected by a human indexer (as in the examples of figure 3-2) or, sometimes, by computer. (See Automatic Methods, later in this chapter, for a discussion of automatic indexing by computer.) Consistency in subject indexing by humans is usually achieved by means of a controlled vocabulary. This, in its simplest form, is merely a list of the terms that the indexer is allowed to use. The fact that the term "adverse effects" appears in such a list implies that the indexer must use this term where appropriate, rather than a possible variant. A slightly more sophisticated controlled vocabulary would include the more important variants as cross references (for example, "side effects *use* adverse effects").

The ideal subject indexing situation would be one in which all aspects of interest can be represented using a rather small vocabulary of terms that can be printed out on a single sheet of paper or displayed in toto on a screen, especially if the terms can be classified in some useful way. For example, figure 3-4 shows a hypothetical vocabulary that might be used by a manufacturer or distributor of toys. A vocabulary of this type tells the indexer what aspects should be covered in the indexing and what terms should be used. Thus, a red pull toy made of a combination of plastic and wood would be indexed under "red," "pull toy," "plastic," "wood," and "2–5." Of course, this is a very simplistic example, and the hypothetical vocabulary is both incomplete and lacking in specificity. Nevertheless, it does illustrate the fact that a very small vocabulary can sometimes be adequate in highly specialized database applications.

Figure 3-4   Partial Vocabulary of Terms Relating to Toys

Material	Age Group	Use
Cloth	Infant	To cuddle
Plastic	2–5	To look at
Wood	6–12	To draw on
Metal	13–18	To move
Paper	Adult	
Rubber		

Color	Locomotion	Shape
Red	Push toy	Spherical
Blue	Pull toy	Cube
Green	Clockwork	Tubular
Yellow	Electric	Square
Brown	Steam	Oblong
Black		Triangular
White		Round
Purple		Flat

In the majority of situations, however, such a small controlled vocabulary will not be adequate, and an alternative form of vocabulary control is needed.

Fortunately, almost all the publishers of the major bibliographic databases have compiled controlled vocabularies, and these can be purchased for use by others. The great majority of these are in the form of thesauri. An information retrieval thesaurus is somewhat different from the more conventional thesaurus designed to group synonyms. The information retrieval thesaurus prescribes the vocabulary to be used for indexing and provides an elaborate cross-reference structure to help indexers choose the best terms, to help users of the database choose the right terms to perform a search, and to lead searchers to all of the terms needed to make the search comprehensive.

Figure 3-5 shows the structure of some sample entries from a hypothetical thesaurus. Words considered sufficiently close to be synonymous are "controlled" by choosing one and referring from the other through the *use* instruction. An indexer may not use the term *cereals* but must instead use the term *grain,* thereby avoiding the situation in which some records bear one term and some the other. Words having more than one meaning, such as "plants," are treated as though they were different words. Terms whose meanings are related are linked together in two

**Figure 3-5   Sample Entries from a Hypothetical Thesaurus
for Information Retrieval**

....

barley
            broader term *grain*

cereals
            use *grain*

corn
            broader term *grain*

factories
            used for *plants (industry)*

grain
            used for *cereals*
            broader term *crops*
            narrower terms *barley*
                                       corn
                                       maize
                                       oats
                                       rye
                                       wheat

            related terms   *flour*
                                      flour mills
                                      harvesting
                                      milling
                                      threshing

plants (botany)

plants (industry)
            use *factories*

....

ways. Those related generically are indicated by "broader term" and "narrower term" listings. As shown, the term *grain* has listed beneath it both the term immediately above it hierarchically (that is, its genus), *crops,* and the terms immediately beneath it hierarchically (that is, its species), namely the individual grain terms. In addition, terms related to *grain* in ways other than a formal genus-species relation (for example, agricultural or industrial operations related to grain) are also displayed. Thus, the searcher (as well as the indexer) is given a complete picture of all terms in the vocabulary that are considered to be related to "grain." This helps both indexer and searcher in selecting the terms most appropriate for a particular situation. In this manner, the thesaurus is able to prevent the separation of related material under synonymous terms, to distinguish words having different meanings, and to give the searcher positive assistance in the conduct of a comprehensive search in the database.

To control the terminology used to index records in a database, then, it may be possible to adopt a thesaurus produced by a major database publisher such as the National Library of Medicine, the National Agricultural Library, the Educational Resources Information Center, or the Institution of Electrical and Electronics Engineers. The vocabularies of such organizations cover entire disciplines: medicine, agriculture, education, and physics/electronics. Other thesauri cover virtually the whole of knowledge at a more superficial level. A good example is the *UNBIS Thesaurus* published by the United Nations. In addition, there exist many thesauri dealing with more specific fields.

In short, an organization wishing to control the vocabulary to be used in indexing its own database would be well advised to see if some published vocabulary is appropriate for this purpose. On the other hand, the interests of the organization may be so specialized that no existing thesaurus would meet its vocabulary needs. This might be so, for example, in the case of the hypothetical toy manufacturer mentioned earlier. In this situation, it may be desirable to create one's own specialized thesaurus. The existing thesauri can be used as models and guides. Texts describing methods of thesaurus construction have also been published. See, for example, books by Lancaster and by Aitchison and others.[1] While it may be time-consuming and costly for an organization to create its own specialized thesaurus, and to keep it current, this may well be justified if the contents of the database are considered sufficiently valuable.

Of course, it is not absolutely essential to control vocabulary used to index. Indexers can simply assign terms freely, drawing the terms from their own experience or, where appropriate, directly from the texts they are indexing. This will be less expensive: The extraction of terms from text can be done by personnel at a clerical level (or perhaps by computer as discussed later in this chapter), while assignment of terms from a thesaurus will usually require that the indexer be reasonably knowledgeable on the subject matter dealt with. In any case, looking terms up in a thesaurus usually takes longer than merely picking words and phrases from the text.

It must be recognized, however, that it is much more difficult to search a database in which the vocabulary used is not subject to any control. Obviously, similar items may be indexed under quite different words, so the user of the database must be able to think of the alternatives. This is especially difficult in a comprehensive search. Returning to figure 3-5, note how the thesaurus tells the searcher all of the terms needed for a search on "grains." It would be tedious and time-consuming to have to think of all these terms. Obviously, there are much worse situations than this. Think how difficult it would be to arrive at all the metal terms needed, for example, in a search for information on effect of metals on the central nervous system.

In short, if the database is judged to be of sufficient value and if it is important to save the time of the users, reduce their frustration, and make them more successful, the expense of controlling the language used to index the contents of the database may well be justified.

Of course, the language occurring in a free-text database (titles, extracts, abstracts, or full text) is not controlled, so the burden is on the user to think of all the ways that an idea may be expressed in natural language. This is not necessarily a trivial task. For example, in the medical literature the idea of "levels (of a substance) in the blood" can be expressed in almost a limitless variety of ways, such as

> blood levels
>
> serum levels
>
> blood concentration
>
> serum concentration
>
> level of . . . in the blood
>
> level of . . . in the serum
>
> concentration in the blood
>
> levels in the blood

This list is by no means complete.

In the case of a text database that reflects an organization's own internal resources (for example, the full text of its research reports), it may be worthwhile to impose some standardization and quality control on the contents even in cases where no indexing is performed. For example, authors of reports can be instructed to make report titles as complete and explicit as possible, and abstracts can be written in such a way that they facilitate retrieval as well as explicating what the report is about or what its findings are. To facilitate retrieval, a good abstract should be long, providing as many useful access points as possible. Redundancy is useful in such an abstract because it improves the chance of retrieval if the same idea is expressed in more than one way.

As stated previously, human indexing can be expensive, especially when a relatively large controlled vocabulary is involved because this will usually mean the use of indexers knowledgeable in the subject. Building and maintaining the controlled vocabulary will also be expensive. As a compromise, however, it is sometimes useful to rely primarily on free text (full text or something less) but to supplement this with use of a *small* controlled vocabulary of rather broad terms that is easy and inexpensive to create and to apply. Such a vocabulary would deal only in broad concepts and would typically include no more than 200 terms. This type of broad categorization serves two useful purposes:

1. It makes it much easier to perform broad searches. For example, the broad term "metals" makes a comprehensive metals search possible without having to think of all possible metals terms.

2. It reduces the possible ambiguity of free text alone. For example, the word "strike," occurring in text, has several possible meanings. This ambiguity can be reduced when the text word is combined with broad subject categories such as "terrorism" or "industrial relations."

Specificity

As discussed previously, the length of a database record (number of access points provided) is a major factor determining its retrievability. Looked at in a somewhat different way, if reasonably comprehensive searches are to be performed in a database, the records must be sufficiently long. At the same time, one wants to avoid a situation in which searches in the database frequently retrieve large numbers of irrelevant items. To reduce this occurrence, the terminology used to represent items in the database must be sufficiently specific.

The terms employed for subject access must be specific enough to allow searches to be performed at a level of detail appropriate to the interests of database users. For example, if a user wants information on teddy bears, he or she may not want everything on cuddly toys and will certainly not want everything on toys in general. For this user, the vocabulary must be more specific than "toys" or even "cuddly toys"; the precise term "teddy bears" is needed. Clearly, the producer of a database must know a considerable amount about the needs and interests of the people likely to use it. The hypothetical vocabulary for toys illustrated in figure 3-4 is not nearly specific enough.

The requirement for specificity applies to databases of all types. The terms used to index statistical compilations must be at a level of specificity appropriate to the search needs of users of these sources, and likewise for the image databases. In the case of bibliographic databases, the specificity requirement applies most obviously to controlled subject terms since text words (in titles and abstracts) will usually be at the level of specificity of the contents of the publication itself. For a database that is searchable on both text words and controlled terms, the requirement for specificity of the latter is less important as long as users can combine the broader controlled terms with the text words to achieve the desired precision.

The effect of specificity on retrieval capabilities is illustrated more dramatically in figure 3-6. Imagine a user wanting to search our toy database for items dealing with cuddly Winnie the Pooh toys. If the records are fully specific, the term "Winnie the Pooh" will occur in all relevant records: The user should be able to retrieve all the relevant records and only relevant ones. As the vocabulary gets less and less specific, however, the search would retrieve more and more records that are completely irrelevant: all teddy bears, all cuddly toys, or even all toys! This particular example illustrates the fact that free text can have certain advantages over controlled vocabularies: The name Winnie the Pooh is likely to occur in the text of relevant items but a controlled vocabulary may be less specific.

Figure 3-6   Effect of Vocabulary Specificity on Retrieval Capability

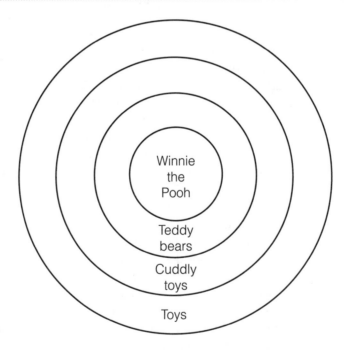

Other Quality Factors

The producers of a database have the responsibility for ensuring that data included are as accurate as possible. Unfortunately, control of the quality of the data is rarely given high priority by database producers. Consequently, high error rates occur in many databases, even the major international ones. For example, inaccuracies in bibliographic references (incorrect volume or issue numbers for journals or incorrect page numbers for articles) may waste the time of users, frustrate them, or cause them needless expense.

Typographical errors are not trivial matters. A user can have little confidence in a database in which many typographical errors occur. Moreover, such errors can have significant effects on search results, causing some records not to be retrieved when they should be and others to be retrieved when they should not be. As many as forty-six different misspellings of a single term have been found in certain databases. Clearly, the chance that searchers would be able to find all records related to this term is very slight indeed.

Every attempt should be made to ensure the quality of abstracts, or other descriptive narratives, to ensure that they accurately reflect the content or character of the items being described. Users of a database will be justifiably annoyed if abstracts are frequently misleading, causing them to seek publications that turn out to be of no interest or, conversely, to overlook items that may be of great interest.

Accuracy of data is not a matter to be taken lightly. Under certain circumstances, publishers can face legal action if incorrect information in a database results in some type of loss to an individual or institution. Database producers should encourage users to report any errors they discover and should be willing to correct any identified errors in updates of the database.

A further responsibility of the database producer is the preparation of an adequate user manual in printed form, accessible online, or both. The manual should give a complete and accurate description of the contents of the database as a whole, as well as the content and format of individual records, and should give clear explanations of how the database can be used, including samples of search approaches. It should also give information on other matters of likely concern to users, such as frequency of updating.

Automatic Methods

As suggested previously, computers can be used to perform certain tasks that usually require human intellectual processing. For example, computers can be used to index text or to summarize it in some way. Programs capable of performing operations of this kind are commercially available, and some can be accessed through the World Wide Web. New products appear frequently and others disappear, so reviews in this area soon become out-of-date. New products are advertised, described, and sometimes evaluated in various trade magazines.

Indexing by Extraction

Given text in electronic form, a computer can extract words or phrases that may be good indicators of what the text is about. The words or phrases thus selected become the searchable access points (index terms) for the text in place of humanly selected access points such as those illustrated earlier in figure 3-2. This is automatic indexing by extraction.

The simplest form of extraction indexing is based solely on word frequency. That is, common words (articles, prepositions, conjunctions) are ignored, but all others are ranked by how frequently they occur. Those words or phrases that occur in the text most often are selected. For the academic boycott article (figure 3-3), this might result in a list looking as follows:

    academic
    academic boycott
    book boycott
    boycott
    libraries
    scholars
    South African
    universities

Since frequency of occurrence is often a good measure of relevance, automatic indexing of this kind can be quite successful: The computer may well extract words and phrases that an intelligent human would select from the text.

Extraction indexing can be more sophisticated than this. For example, extraction programs can be written to ignore words or phrases that occur frequently in the text but also occur frequently in the database as a whole. Thus, if the entire database were about South Africa, the expression "South African" would not be selected. On the other hand, words or phrases that occur very rarely in the database are selected even if they do not appear frequently in the text at hand. Thus, in the boycott example, "Trinity College" might be selected for the simple reason that it has never occurred before.

Software for extraction indexing may also take other criteria into account, such as position in text: Words in titles, section headings, and perhaps other locations may be given more weight in the selection process than other words are given.

In special forms of extraction indexing, the selection programs search for and extract text of a particular type, such as names of individuals or names of organizations.

Assignment Indexing

Computers can also be used to put text into particular preselected categories. This is sometimes referred to as *assignment indexing* because index terms (or category codes) are assigned to the text by the computer. Programs that do this operate by matching the words in the text with words associated with the categories to be assigned. A category (term) is assigned when the text words match the word profile of the category sufficiently well. For example, the profile for the category "higher education" might include such words or phrases as "universities," "colleges," "faculty," "professors," and "academic" as well as "higher education" itself. This category might thus be assigned to the article on academic boycotts since these words or phrases occur frequently in the text.

In general, this type of text categorization (or classification) is machine-aided rather than completely automatic. Since the programs will sometimes assign categories incorrectly or fail to assign a category that should be recognized, the automatic categorization is usually validated by humans.

Automated Summarization

Using the same types of criteria used for automatic indexing, programs can also be used to compile extracts automatically. An extract of this kind is a series of sentences selected by computer from the full text. The sentences thus selected should be those most likely to illustrate what the full text is about. This usually means that the sentences selected are those that contain the greatest concentration of the high-frequency words. Since the sentences thus extracted can appear in quite different parts of the complete text, the resulting extract is unlikely to read as smoothly as a humanly prepared abstract would, but it might still be a good indicator of what the full text deals with. While the more sophisticated programs can do clever things, such as combining two adjacent sentences while eliminating redundancy, they cannot produce summaries of the same quality as humanly prepared abstracts.

One special form of text summarization combines extraction and categorization. The programs prepared for this purpose will look for particular words or phrases in text or particular types of text (for example, names), extract these, and put them into a preestablished template. The result is a kind of structured abstract. For example, the text of newspapers or news feeds can be scanned for mentions of executives changing positions. The information thus identified and extracted can then be put into a preestablished structure (the template), which might look somewhat as follows.

Executive: Michael Pringle

Previous position: Vice President, Marketing

Previous employer: ABC Corp.

New position: Executive Vice President

New employer: XYZ Corp.

Date: 5/13/97

The simplest of automatic procedures, based on extraction from text, are inexpensive and capable of producing acceptable representations of the text. The automatic assignment of preestablished categories is a more expensive proposition because the category profiles must be updated frequently, which can be very costly when many hundreds or thousands of categories are involved. This more costly procedure is unlikely to be fully automatic because human review will usually be necessary. While automatic indexing and extracting procedures can be satisfactory for many purposes, they are unlikely to produce representations of the same quality as those prepared by skilled indexers and abstractors.

Special Applications

The factors that affect quality apply to databases of any kind, although they relate most obviously to bibliographic or text databases. Special types of databases or special applications may present differences in detail but not in principle. In the case of a statistical database, for example, the labels given to the numerical data must be unambiguous, and they should be controlled and standardized. Image databases present no real differences in cases in which the image depicted is described in verbal form (true of the great majority), although they may offer some unconventional indexing problems. For example, a database of paintings may involve the use of terms that represent a variety of characteristics: the things depicted, the colors involved, spatial relationships, and so on. The quality and usability principles still apply: The more complete the description, the more precise and standardized the terminology, the more effectively the database can be exploited. Even the (relatively few) image databases that are designed to be searched primarily through a form of pattern matching (for example, find a painting that looks like this sketch) are governed by the same principles, although somewhat in reverse—since it is the completeness and preciseness of the pattern used to interrogate the database that will most significantly affect retrieval.

The more demanding the use made of the database, the more important become the principles of quality and usability. A system designed to answer questions directly will require more complete and precise indexing than one designed to retrieve a source that may contain an answer; *data mining* applications (that is, use of programs that look for hidden patterns or associations among data) will require the use of records that are as complete and detailed as possible. For example, medical records designed to be used in data mining applications must include more complete and detailed information about patients, diagnoses, therapies, and outcomes than records maintained for less stringent and sophisticated uses.

The less conventional types of databases referred to in this section are likely to pose special requirements for record formats and database structures. These topics, among others, are dealt with in Part II of the book.

Note   1. F. W. Lancaster, *Vocabulary Control for Information Retrieval,* 2d ed. (Arlington, Va.: Information Resources, 1986); Jean Aitchison, Alan Gilchrist, and David Bawden, *Thesaurus Construction and Use: A Practical Manual,* 3d ed. (London: Aslib, 1997).

PART II

Software
Issues

4

Types of Database Software

Numerous software options are available for building your own database. These have a wide ranging set of capabilities. Price is not necessarily an indicator of performance. For example, one of the most capable programs, Micro-CDS/ISIS of UNESCO, is available free for nonprofit purposes to organizations in member states of UNESCO through national or regional distributors. This is a particularly relevant and appropriate program for some of the applications discussed in Part I, such as the creation of a database of articles, books, and conference papers related to the key products of a developing country or the national bibliography of a small country.

Ideally, software should be chosen to match the type of database to be developed. This matching is part of the database feasibility study well illustrated through case studies and explained in detail by Tenopir and Lundeen.[1] In reality, the software choice is often determined by two overriding conditions: the price of the software and the familiarity of the person(s) involved in building a database with the software alternatives available. Using a simple relational database management program for a national bibliography is not impossible, but it is like offering fine wine in a paper cup. Such an application can be much better handled with software designed from the ground up for managing highly structured bibliographic information with multiple field values (for authors, subject headings), special filing rules (for titles starting with definite or indefinite articles), and a variety of index creation options (for keywords, authors, titles, publishers, and their combinations) through inverted (index) files.

On the other hand, the circulation file of a small library begs for a program that uses relational database management techniques. In a relational database, independent files are linked through unique keys on demand. For example, in a circulation system there is a rather simple file for each patron that includes the first name, last name, and unique ID of the patron and another simple file for each copy of a book that includes the book title, the ISBN, and the copy number. When a patron borrows a book, his or her unique ID is entered in the book file; when the book is returned, the patron ID is removed from the book file. The link between the book and patron file is the patron ID. There might be other files that include more details about the patron or the book, but these are not required for routine transactions. However, if the patron's address is needed to send an availability notice, the simple patron file may be linked to the complete patron file that includes the patron's address, phone number, and other personal data. The link between the simple and complete patron file would be the patron ID.

Relational database management software is the appropriate tool for handling constantly changing links between items and patrons. Bibliographic sophistication is not required for circulation systems, such as filing a book under its uniform title or providing a cross reference from the author's pen name to the real name. The patron already has the item in hand, and even if she doesn't have her library card ready, she can confirm the correct spelling of her name for the borrowing transaction.

The Components of a Database

Various approaches can be used to describe the components of a database and the relationship among those components. A large body of literature about the underlying concepts, organization, and structure of databases exists. A few highly relevant books are cited throughout this chapter for those who would like to learn more about the structural and conceptual issues of databases. This book deals with these technical development issues only to the extent necessary for evaluating and selecting software for creating in-house those types of databases discussed in Part I. Following are some working definitions of basic terms used in this and the remaining chapters.

Database

A database is the collection of electronic records about entities. The entities may be books, journal articles, stamps, videotapes, borrowers, associations, etc. The collection of information on one type of entity is a file. In relational database management programs, this file is called a *table*.

Record

Within the file the information about one entity is referred to as a record. The records make a file. In relational database management systems, a record is represented by a row in a table.

Fields

The units of information that describe a specific characteristic of the entity are attributes. For a journal article the attributes may include—among others—the title and subtitle of the article, author, title and subtitle of the journal, its ISSN, volume and issue identifiers, pagination, and any other chronological and numerical designation data. These attributes are the fields of a record and the columns of a table. The fields are identified by a field name (author, title, subtitle, or ISSN), a tag (AU:, TI:, ST:, and SN: or AU-, TI-, ST-, and SN-), or a field number (100, 245, 121, 022, etc.).

Subfields

Sophisticated textual database management systems can split the fields into subfields that are identified by a subfield delimiter (symbol) and a subfield code (letter or number) such as %b or $b or ^b for a subtitle. Columns in tables are not further subdivided into subcolumns. A subfielded name field may look like this:

^aSinatra^bFrank^d1915-1998

The subfield delimiters (^, %, and $ are the most common) vary from program to program. Also varying are subfield codes and whether punctuation marks are included with the subfields or added when the records are displayed or printed.

A (sub)field or column value is typically the smallest unit of information (data with meaning for humans), and it consists of characters. For humans the entire character string makes sense; for the program, individual characters are the smallest units of processing. Occasionally, a single character may represent meaningful data, such as the letters S and F for the status of a patron (student or faculty) or the number 8 that may represent the issue number of a journal or the maximum number of items a patron may borrow.

Indicators

Single-character information carriers that modify or qualify the (sub)field that follows them are called indicators. For example, the first indicator of the title proper field provides information about the number of characters at the beginning of a title that should be ignored for sorting. For example,

4_The Wizard of Oz

indicates that the first four characters must be ignored in sorting, so that the record appears under W. The second indicator has a blank in our example. Indicators are used only in the most demanding bibliographic databases (such as national catalogs) that exchange and process records in MARC (*MA*chine *R*eadable *C*ataloging) Communications format. Only the most specialized library programs are capable of handling indicators.

Field Values

Values are assigned to the fields (attributes) of each record (entity). The set of attribute values or field values that describe the entity distinguishes one entity from the other. Not all attributes are applicable to all the entities. One book may have a subtitle; another may not. One may have an editor; the other may not. The field values may be classified by type as numeric, alphabetic, alphanumeric, date, currency, etc.

The more attributes used and the more attribute values assigned, the more distinguishable an item becomes. If only a few attributes are used, and if not all attribute values are assigned, two entities may seem to the user to be identical (such as the normal and letter-box edition of a video movie or the original and the revised edition of a book). Internally, however, entities are identified by a record number. This number can be assigned automatically by the software, by the data entry operator, or by the person who created the original record for the document.

The following two figures (4-1 and 4-2) illustrate the differences between a simple, moderately structured record and a highly structured record of the Library of Congress in labeled MARC format. The simple record may be appropriate for a circulation system, the MARC format record for a catalog in an academic library. Note that not even the most granular (deeply structured) record structure is a guarantee for accurate content. It is ironic that the first name of Wilfrid Lancaster is entered incorrectly as Wilfred twice in the same record in figure 4-2.

The simple record in figure 4-1 has 17 fields, some of them purely alphabetic, such as the circulation type, copy status, and inventory status. Some are purely numeric, such as the copy number; some are numeric in currency format (price); and some are alphanumeric (bar code). The call number field seems to be alphabetic in this case, but it is alphanumeric to accommodate call numbers that have letters, numbers, and special characters.

The title field is not structured. Unless one knows these classic short stories of Sherlock Holmes, it is not clear if there are two novels in this

Figure 4-1   Simple Bibliographic Record for a Circulation System

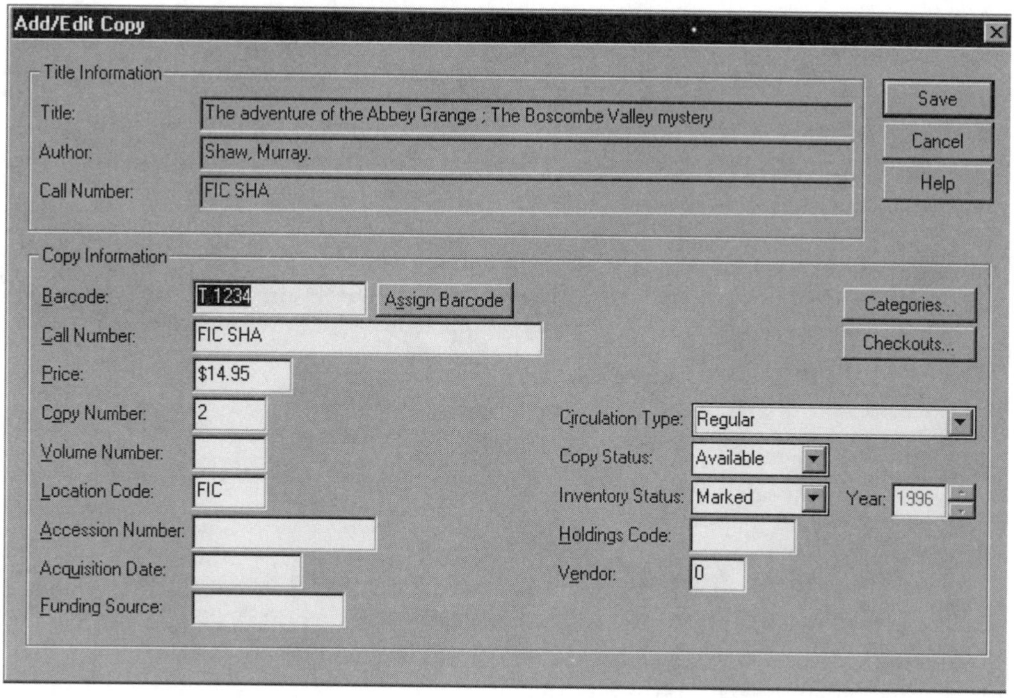

work or if "The Boscombe Valley Mystery" is the subtitle. The author field is not unambiguous, though the punctuation (and part of the call number field) makes it clear for the literate patron that Shaw is the last name and Murray is the first name. (Actually, Murray Shaw is an adapter of the Arthur Conan Doyle short stories.)

The record in figure 4-2 is deeply structured. Beyond the field types discussed for the simple bibliographic record, this record has subfields and indicators. The title field, for example, is split into subfield $a for title proper and subfield $c for statement of responsibility. All the other fields are deeply structured, consisting of two or three subfields. Subfield $a in the author name field is the personal name, subfield $q is the fuller form of the name (and both have Wilfrid misspelled as Wilfred), and subfield $d is the date associated with the name, typically used to distinguish authors with identical names.

All fields in figure 4-2 have two positions for indicators, though in this example few are used. The underscored character means that the value of the indicator is a space. There are many uses for the indicators. The same indicator value may have different meaning for the different

Figure 4-2   Labeled MARC Record for a Catalog

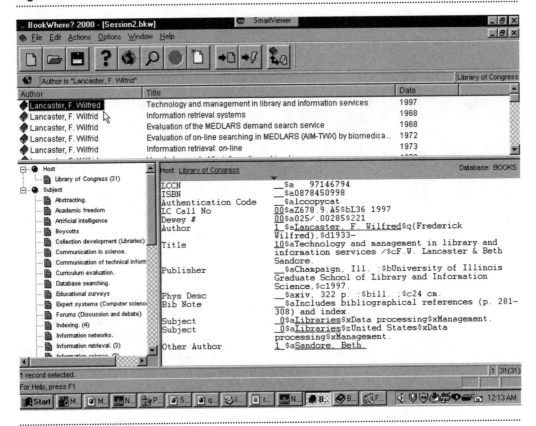

fields. In the case of the author, for example, the value of the first indicator (1) indicates that the last name is a single surname. The second indicator (_) indicates that no subject entry should be generated for the name of the person. The first indicator (1) in the title field indicates that a title added entry should be generated from the title field, while the second indicator (0) indicates that no characters should be ignored in sorting. This indicator would have the value of 4 for a title like *The Beauty of the MARC Format* to indicate that the first four characters should be ignored in sorting. Why four characters? The space following the definite article *(The)* should be ignored, too. The same indicator pair (1_) is used for the other author in the Author added (labeled as Other Author) field. (These labels use the layperson's terms instead of the MARC terminology to appear less intimidating.)

Categories of Database Software

The combination of files makes up a database. Unfortunately, many programs use the terms *file* and *database* interchangably. "Databases" that consist of a single file typically should not be called databases. The file created by a word processor for the collection of records that describe the books on order is simply a book order file. If it has one or more index files by, say, publisher name, ISBN, and requestor that point back to records in the order file, it is a book order database that can be searched by publisher, ISBN, and requestor.

In the case of most programs, the files that make up a database are identified externally for users. A Micro-CDS/ISIS database consists of eight to ten component files. A DB/TextWorks database is made of a minimum of ten files. A ProCite database consists of two files. The number of files that are identifiable by the operating system through their distinct names should not be used to judge if the program is a database management or a simple file handling program. One of the best relational database management programs, FileMaker Pro 4.0, packs all of the components in a single file. Internally, however, that file has different components (data entry templates, master records, index entries, authority files, etc.) identifiable only by the application software but not by the operating system.

The internal structure of the relations and the techniques used to establish those relations among the files create different types of databases. From the 1990s, relational and inverted databases have become predominant. From the functional point of view, distinctions can be made between generic database management software and text management software that specializes to handle textual information, as explained in the following sections.

Generic Database Management Software

Generic database management software (Paradox, dBASE, FoxPro, Approach) is often used to create relational databases for library applications. Such database management systems have as their advantage the ability to handle—with some significant limitations—both textual and numeric data and to provide not only information storage and retrieval functions but also arithmetic functions (such as totaling the spent and encumbered budget by departments or by the branches of the library). Lately, these database management programs have been enhanced to handle images, sound files, and video clips in digital format.

Text Management Software

Textual information management software packages (Inmagic, Micro-CDS/ISIS) excel in storing, retrieving, sorting, and displaying textual information, but with a few exceptions, they cannot do arithmetic operations beyond searching for fields whose values are larger than a specified number, such as for publishing year greater than 1998 (PY>1998). The latest versions of text management software (such as DB/TextWorks) now can handle images or even image, video, and sound files (WinISIS). These can enhance textual information and allow the storage of graphics, charts, and illustrations.

Most textual information management software packages use master files and inverted files to link records with index terms. Inverted files act like indexes to the records in the master file. There are significant differences in the amount and detail of information stored in the index files of different programs; these in turn will define the search capabilities.

If the inverted file does not include information about the source of origin of a term (such as the title field, or the series statement) or about the position of the term within the title field, it is not possible to do field-specific, positional, and proximity searches. (These searches are discussed in chapter 8.)

Programming Databases

Both generic database management software and text management software have to be programmed by the developer of the application to provide the required functions. This programming may involve writing actual instructions following the syntax specifications of the software, but usually it involves providing parameters, often in coded format, to specify the choice and mode of indexing, for example. An instruction to create an index entry with the FT= prefix from each occurrence of subfield ^t of field 780 (former title) may look like this in Micro-CDS/ISIS:

780 0 mhu, (|FT=|v780^t/)

Such an instruction doesn't exactly roll off the tongue of the developers of applications unless they study the documentation and spend some time with the program. A series of such statements will define the content of the index entries. Defining the display and print formats requires similar programming statements with conditional operations that are skipped or executed based on the presence or absence of a field or of a field value, such as a series number or the name of a series editor.

Most of the Macintosh and Windows software for information storage and retrieval try to facilitate the programming aspect of creating a database by offering a series of templates, pull-down and pop-up menus, check boxes, and counter boxes to allow the developer to provide the instructions without learning the syntax rules of the underlying program. These graphical tools include intuitive screen drawing and painting features to design the layout of data entry and output screens, templates for data entry validation and indexing, and pop-up windows to specify sort and print format preferences. With the advent of graphical user interfaces the programming aspects become more and more transparent. Examples are shown in chapters 9 and 10.

From the end users many of these software packages require only that users enter a query, press function keys or buttons, or select check boxes on templates to change sort preferences or to customize the printed output by including their name, the date, and the topic of their searches.

Turnkey Software

Those who want to have out-of-the-box convenience may choose preprogrammed (also known as turnkey) software packages for specific library and information center applications such as serials control, cataloging, circulation, acquisitions, or bibliography preparation. Some of the turnkey programs are dedicated to one task, but most of them provide a suite of programs for several functions. These can be bought as individual modules or as an integrated package.

Some turnkey software packages are based on generic database management systems, but most are written directly in a programming language, such as Visual C or Pascal. After a quick and easy installation, these programs are ready to accept records to create a database. They offer several transaction-management options, such as placing orders and sending claims or overdue notices. They may allow some minimal customization by offering user-defined fields, but compared with generic database management and text management programs they are like ready-made clothes versus tailor-made ones.

Advantages and Disadvantages of Software Categories

There has been remarkable convergence among the three types of alternatives in the 1990s. Traditional textual information management programs have been endowed with built-in numeric functions that may outperform those found in general database management systems. This is the case with DB/TextWorks; it combines the best of inverted file and relational database techniques and treats text and crunches numbers with aplomb.

Micro-CDS/ISIS supplies a full-blown programming language, ISIS-Pascal, to enhance its impressive indexing, sorting, and print-formatting capabilities. Relational database management programs have been improved to manage sophisticated text functions. For example, FileMaker Pro 4.0 has impressive authority-control functions to improve data entry consistency. Authority-control functions make it easy to create and update lists of validated names and codes and compare these lists with the content of the fields as they are being typed in. Authority files are mostly used for such fields as author names, uniform titles, subject headings, corporate names, journal titles, and country names. The prepackaged citation style formats of ProCite's latest version released in early 1998 have been enhanced by a quite sophisticated and customizable duplicate detection option.

Despite this convergence, there are distinct advantages for each category of database management software packages for textual information handling. Mainstream generic database management programs are not ideal for applications in which strict adherence to cataloging rules is required, such as in public access catalogs.

These database management programs use fixed-length fields (columns); therefore, the designer must contemplate the longest possible value of an attribute because many data elements, such as the title proper field, cannot be abbreviated or truncated. Neither can they easily accommodate fields that may have multiple values (such as several descriptors) unless they include a predefined number of columns for the maximum number of descriptors. This may result in wasted storage and inefficient processing of data when an entity (record) can have from one to seventeen descriptors. Traits such as these must be analyzed on a case-by-case basis because FileMaker Pro, for example, handles repeatable fields easily even though it is a relational database management program.

Bibliography management software packages are ideal for those who need to produce bibliographies in compliance with the ever-increasing number of citation styles of publishers, societies, and associations. However, the predefined templates of these packages may not provide enough flexibility to include all data elements required for the complete and adequate description of, say, a collection of CD-ROM databases in a library. Neither may they offer authority control for several data elements in a bibliographic record. Their search capabilities also may be limited.

Textual information management programs may be able to handle various diacritical characters and filing rules in displaying bibliographic records sorted by hierarchical criteria (by publisher, then title, then year). However, they may not be able to recalculate the budget for the Asia collection of standing orders for Thai, Korean, and Japanese serials after the plummeting of the baht, won, and yen.

Hardware and Operating System Platforms

It is still the exception rather than the rule to have the same software available for both the Macintosh and the IBM-compatible platform. In principle, the choice of software ideal for the application should determine the hardware to be acquired. In reality, the hardware environment may be a given, and it may limit the choice, especially for Macintosh users. Among the often-mentioned programs in this book, DB/TextWorks, Micro-CDS/ISIS, and Reference Manager are available only for IBMs and compatible PCs.

The hardware defines to a large extent the operating system platform. For IBM users—especially in the Windows environment—there are several alternatives. DOS is on its way out as an application platform. For example, Library Master is one of the few major bibliography management programs that still develops the DOS version and does not yet have a Windows version. (However, a Windows version may be available later in 1998, and Library Master runs in a DOS box under Windows.) Most of the developers of integrated software packages focus their development efforts for the Windows platform to make the applications more user friendly. The WinISIS version of Micro-CDS/ISIS introduced in 1997 will give a boost to application developments as both the database definition and the retrieval aspects of this powerhouse software have been simplified immensely in the Windows version.

The Macintosh platform has always offered intuitive products for both designers and end users. Claris Corporation (FileMaker, Inc., since 1998) made database design and information retrieval intuitive while developers and especially users still struggled with DOS applications. The Windows version of FileMaker Pro clearly shows the traits of its Macintosh origin and offers the ultimate in user friendliness. Still, the mismanagement of Apple in the '90s took its toll. As this book goes to press, Intuit, Inc., announced that it will not offer the Macintosh version of its very popular personal finance management software. It is clear that software developers are moving toward Windows 95/98 and Windows NT. Sooner or later they will not enhance their DOS and Windows 3.x versions, and the Macintosh software market is likely to shrink further except in a few applications areas, which are unlikely to include textual information management.

The popularity of the World Wide Web has brought along a number of new retrieval engines that can be deployed on the Web. Most of them require that the Internet Service Provider authorize the database publisher to use Common Gateway Interface (CGI) scripts. More importantly, these Web retrieval tools presume that a database is already in existence. Most databases are created off the Web, using traditional desktop database creation tools that are then loaded to a Web site or, more often, linked to a Web site. (Database creation should not be confused with Web site management or with Web site management tools. They complement each other.) Currently, CGI and Java applications focus on the retrieval aspects of textual information management and, to a lesser extent, on the aspects of porting legacy databases—those that have been developed decades earlier on mainframes and personal computers—to the Web environment.

Selection of the Best Alternative

One should not have prejudices against any of the database management categories. The characteristic features of the application to be automated should decide which category of database management program may be the most appropriate. The types of databases identified in chapter 1 can be implemented using different categories of software.

Some of the criteria to be discussed in the following chapters are more relevant for full-text databases, others for bibliographic databases built predominantly from imported records. Most of the criteria apply whether you want to create a desktop database, a CD-ROM database for distribution, or a Web database to be published on the Internet or an intranet.

The criteria and the tools for CD-ROM and Web database building are practically the same as for the desktop database building. It is the distribution and online serving aspects that present additional and unique criteria such as the need for and capabilities of CD-ROM premastering software, Web server software, and the legal and financial aspects of publishing data and of distributing the run-time version of software. These allow users to search the database, sort, print, and download records but not to edit the records or to define or change database structure or indexing. (These aspects are beyond the scope of this book and belong to the domain of publishing and distributing databases.)

An acquisitions system (a specific type of bibliographic database) does not need to follow AACR2 rules to the letter, but it should be able to offer decent search capabilities, to handle the budget as new items are ordered and others are fulfilled, and to handle business transactions. A simple business database management program could do the job well. Even the current generation of spreadsheet software might be used because these now offer modest search capabilities. The programming of generic database management software is not discussed in this book. Readers interested in the programming aspects of library applications using generic database management software such as dBASE should refer to the excellent tutorial of Yerkey.[2]

An online public access catalog of books, serials, maps, and audiovisual materials (another specific type of the bibliographic database genre) does not need to be capable of performing mathematical operations but is expected to handle full records and comply with standards for a variety of document types featuring the peculiarities of a variety of languages. Only sophisticated text management software can be expected to do a quality job for such an application.

A circulation item file does not necessarily need to accommodate all the special Hungarian, Polish, Czech, Danish, and Hawaiian characters that are not part of the extended ASCII character set. Again, a mainstream database management system could be deployed to establish the temporary link between patrons and the items when a book is borrowed, put on hold, or recalled. However, a more appropriate approach would be to purchase a turnkey circulation system for $2,000 that has been thoroughly documented, tested by thousands of users, and reviewed in trade journals and that comes with built-in loan transactions management and customizable recall and availability notices. There is no reason to reinvent the wheel and contract the talented neighbor of the librarian for a possibly never-ending job that is likely to remain a half-baked product with bugs and with no formal support a few years and a few thousand dollars later.

Useful Resources

Matching the requirements of the user and the characteristics of the applications with the features of the software are the keys to selecting the most appropriate software. This is done in the framework of systems analysis that should be the premise for every major information automation project. Tenopir and Lundeen provide the classic treatise of feasibility studies for creating textual databases.[3] The revised edition of Osborne and Nakamura's book is a good source as well.[4] It explains and demonstrates systems analysis applied to library automation projects that replace manual systems. Fidel's book discusses data requirement analysis for systems that do not yet exist and, therefore, that do not replace or complement existing systems.[5] Her book and the one by Bowers provide excellent background for those interested in the underlying concepts and principles of relational databases.[6]

There are unique needs in automating certain functions. The special requirements for specific applications such as calculating grace periods for loan transactions, handling partial payments of fines in a circulation system, or claiming a particular copy of a journal ordered in multiple copies are not discussed here. Instead, see Breeding's well-structured and informative guide to integrated library systems for information about these aspects of library management software.[7] Those interested in learning about the use of ProCite, a capable and widely used bibliography management program, will find the collection of ProCite case studies along with its comprehensive bibliography of this genre of software to be an excellent source.[8] Further background reading includes Crawford's classic book, which makes learning about MARC records a pleasurable experience.[9]

Purchase or License?

Features of software bundled with commercially available CD-ROM databases are discussed in detail by Jacsó, primarily from the perspective of the user interface and information retrieval capabilities.[10] These software packages usually cannot be licensed by those who create the database content. Typically, the software producer licenses the data from the content provider and publishes it as a database, and the two entities split the revenue. The same applies to mainframe software that is used by large online information services such as Dialog Corporation, Ovid Technologies, and Lexis-Nexis. They don't license their software to third parties who want to create an online database, but they do license data files from their creators for online and CD-ROM publishing.

Price   Prices and functional capabilities of database software keep changing. Although references to the latest releases of particular software products are provided (as of spring 1998) here, understand that a new release of the software may enhance the feature set of a program and may eliminate a limitation discussed. For example, version 8.5 of Reference Manager came right on the heels of version 8.0, which had been released a few months before.

The prices of the software vary widely, ranging from the free Micro-CDS/ISIS to software that may cost thousands of dollars. (Micro-CDS/ISIS is a member of the CDS/ISIS family of mainframe, mini-, and microcomputer programs developed for bibliographic information management. The latest incarnation of the micro version is called WinISIS. This book will discuss the micro version [Micro-CDS/ISIS]. When specific features available only under the Windows version are discussed, the term WinISIS will be used.) The typical commercial software needed for building a sophisticated database carries a price tag between $300 and $400 for a single-user version. However, dramatic price reductions can occur almost overnight. For example, one of the most powerful textual information management programs, Insight software from Enigma Corporation, used to cost a whopping $20,000. It was priced out of the reach of many potential users. In 1997 the price was reduced to $7,500—a more affordable price tag, though still on the high end of the spectrum. Micro-CDS/ISIS is the only freeware for qualified organizations.

Network licensing, site licensing, and bundling of the retrieval module with a database for distribution are subject to special pricing. Typically, surcharges apply to any of these categories of use, though the license may authorize the free distribution of run-time version of the retrieval module with databases. For example, DB/TextWorks' license includes the free bundling of DB/SearchWorks. Such pricing strategies are also constantly changing and should be verified with the vendor. See appendix A for a list of URLs for the vendors whose products are mentioned in the book. Many of them offer a demonstration version that can be used to create a small database of 30 to 50 records or to test the software for 30 days. Your best bet is to get the demonstration versions and put them through their paces when it's time to purchase software to build your own database.

This book focuses on explaining and illustrating the importance of the most useful data entry, importing, indexing, retrieval, sorting, output, and interface features of the software that may be needed for computerized textual information management in a library or information center setting. Most of the criteria are applicable to the previously discussed categories of software. These software packages can be purchased or licensed by potential database developers.

It is important to realize that licensing software does not necessarily allow the distribution of the software with the user database. Usually, a so-called run-time version—that allows the searching of the database but not its modification or the creation of new records—can be licensed for an extra charge. The charge may depend on the number of copies or may be based on the number of different databases with which it will be distributed. It may apply for a limited or unlimited period. Inmagic's policy of bundling a free run-time version is very unusual and laudable.

Notes   1. Carol Tenopir and Gerald Lundeen, *Managing Your Information: How to Design and Create a Textual Database on Your Microcomputer* (New York: Neal-Schuman, 1988).

2. A. Neil Yerkey, *Information Management Using dBASE* (New York: Neal-Schuman, 1991).

3. Tenopir and Lundeen.

4. Larry N. Osborne and Margaret Nakamura, *Systems Analysis for Librarians and Information Professionals* (Englewood, Colo.: Libraries Unlimited, 1998).

5. Raya Fidel, *Database Design for Information Retrieval* (New York: John Wiley and Sons, 1987).

6. D. S. Bowers, *From Data to Database* 2d ed. (New York: Chapman and Hall, 1993).

7. Marshall Breeding, *PC-Based Integrated Library Systems* (Westport, Conn.: Meckler, 1994).

8. Deb Renee Biggs, ed., *ProCite in Libraries* (Medford, N.J.: Learned Information, 1995).

9. Walt Crawford, *MARC for Library Use* (Boston: G. K. Hall, 1989).

10. Péter Jacsó, *CD-ROM Software, Dataware and Hardware* (Englewood, Colo.: Libraries Unlimited, 1992).

5

Record and Database Structuring and Data Entry

Versatile structuring of a database into records, fields, and possibly sub-fields is a primary software-selection criterion. Fine structuring of records makes it possible for the database designer to identify the smallest record information elements and their relationship to other elements. The ability of the software to compartmentalize (break down) data has an impact on the effectiveness and efficiency of data entry, indexing, searching, sorting, and output formatting. The more granular the record structure, the more flexible the design process can be.

Structure of Data Fields

Ultimately, the sort and output requirements define how granular the record structure should be. For example, if you need to sort the results by publisher name, then this data element must appear in its own field or subfield. Although it is easy for the human eye to distinguish the three elements of place, publisher, and year in an imprint statement, the delimiting punctuation is not always unambiguous enough to let the program recognize the components. In the following example of an ALA imprint, it is easy to see that the colon delimits the place of publication field and the comma delimits the name of the publisher. However, in the case of a compound publisher name such as Farrar, Straus & Giroux or in a name that includes *Inc.,* such as Information Today, Inc., the delimiters are not unambiguous to a program.

For data entry operations it would not make much difference if the entire imprint statement were entered into a single field, such as

Chicago: American Library Association, 1999

or into three separate fields for place (PL), publisher (PU), and publishing year (PY), as

> PL: Chicago
> PU: American Library Association
> PY: 1999

or into a subfielded field such as

> 260$aChicago$bAmerican Library Association$c1999

However, there are relatively minor implications of the choices. The first option (using one field) may be somewhat more efficient as there is no need to move from one field to another during data entry; therefore, fewer keyboard actions or mouse clicks are required than in the alternative of three separate fields. When thousands of records are entered, such a seemingly minor ergonomic issue of data entry may become an important point and a factor in reducing carpal tunnel syndrome. The subfielded entry has the single field simplicity of the first alternative, but it is not conducive to visual error checking.

Additional differences among the three alternatives exist when indexing and searching. If a word index is created for each word in the imprint field, all three data elements (place of publication, publisher name, and year of publication) can become searchable. Typically, when using the first alternative (one entry), it is not possible for the software to index only the name of the publisher and the publication year because they cannot be unambiguously distinguished from the other components of the imprint field. Usually, the index terms would be put in the publisher index field to make them searchable with a prefix, such as PU=(American and Library and Association) or PB:American w/1 Library w/1 Association, depending on what prefixes and which search operators are used by the software. Consequently, no distinction can be made in searching for "London" as the place of publication and the "Jack London Estate" as the publisher. Such coincidences may be minimal, although in the Library of Congress Web catalog that offers searching by publisher, there is no way to distinguish between ALA, the American Library Association as a publisher, and Ala, the frequently used abbreviation for Alabama, as a place. Hundreds of irrelevant records are retrieved because the publisher index also includes the place of publishing subfield. As mentioned before, a program may be able to extract a character string that it finds between a comma and a semicolon, such as the name of the publisher in our example. This is not only a very rare feature, but it is also a risky option. Given the punctuation inconsistencies in the hundreds of thousands of contributed records in the online utilities, it is obvious that these delimiter characters would not unambiguously identify the publisher component of the imprint field.

Indexing the entire field as a phrase (PU=Chicago: American Library Association, 1999) would not be a smart idea because users could search for a publisher's name only if they know the place of publication, an unlikely assumption. Even if they knew the place of publication, the entries may be scattered due to inconsistent data entries. The entry for another book published by the same publisher in the same year could be hundreds of entries away. For example, "PU=Chicago, IL: American Library Association, 1999" would be followed by the entry "PU=Chicago, IL: Zimanco, Inc., 1950" and far away from the entry "PU=Chicago: American Library Association, 1998" because the latter entry does not have the comma after the city and does not have the state code.

From the aspect of storage requirements, the inability to skip the place of publication component of the imprint field during indexing if this is an unlikely search criterion may also result in wasted space. However, with hard drive capacities in gigabytes, this may not be an important issue.

From the output and sorting perspectives, the ability to distinguish each data element is essential. If a bibliography must be sorted by name of publisher as a primary sort criterion and by year of publication as a secondary search criterion within publisher name, then only the second or third alternatives as shown in the preceding indexing example (with three fields or with subfields) are acceptable.

The subfielded structure is the most sophisticated of the alternatives because it allows the handling of the imprint statement as a single unit for display or print purposes. It also offers the distinct handling of one or more components of the elements of the imprint data group for indexing, sorting, display, and print purposes. For example, the designer may choose the $b (American Library Association) subfield and $c (1999) subfield for indexing, the $c subfield for primary sorting of the results, and all three subfields ($a, $b, and $c) for a full-catalog record display and the second and third subfields for a short-entry print catalog.

Beyond library automation programs for online public access catalogs and serials control, only a few software packages, such as CDS/ISIS, support the subfielded structure. This is an essential feature for those who want to create a database from MARC records with direct import from an earlier system or from the freely available catalogs on the Web that offer MARC export format.

Maximum Number of Data Fields

In the previous examples of imprint-statement entries, support for the second alternative, that of three fields (PL: Chicago; PU: American Library Association; PY: 1999), seems straightforward because most programs allow database designers to define fields to their liking. In reality, designers may be constrained by the limited number of fields the software supports. In the example, three fields would be needed. If there is also a separate copyright date field, the number of fields would increase to four. In our example, the field would look like this:

260$aChicago$bAmerican Library Association$c1999$dcopyright 1998

With the subfielded option, only a new subfield is needed. Because subfield codes are one character long, the twenty-six alphabetic characters and the ten digits provide ample subfield code options. Reference Manager, for example, offers thirty-three fields, and it is easy to hit this limit. For a sophisticated application, fields easily add up to reach the limit. For example, in the case of conference papers, beyond the run-of-the-mill fields about individual papers (record type, record identifier, title, authors, affiliation, reprint address, language, descriptors, classification codes, abstract, pagination, illustrations, references, etc.), records may devour additional fields fast. In this example, extra fields are needed for the title, editor(s), chronological and numerical designation, ISBN or ISSN, publisher, place of publication, and publication year of the proceedings and for the name, city, state, country, sponsor, and date of the conference. In total, an additional twelve to fifteen fields may be needed, depending on how granular the designer wants to make the record structure.

Multiple Types of Records

Being able to use only a small number of fields can be a particularly pressing problem if the program supports only one record type. A single-record format has to accommodate fields for different types of documents that have many unique attributes, such as those required for maps, serials, computer files, and music and video recordings. If the common elements (title, author, publication year, etc.) and the unique elements (parallel, former, successor, alternate, and spine titles; hardware and software requirements; type and format of medium; and composer, conductor, performer, director, producer, etc.) are to be accommodated in a single record type, a program that supports hundreds of fields or an unlimited number of fields may be the only alternative.

Maximum Length of Fields and Records

Restrictions on the length of data fields have been common in software until quite recently. Although limitations such as a maximum of 256 characters per field may not be a problem for most of the data elements, it poses a problem for such fields as abstracts and content notes, which may require thousands of characters. Such a limitation is obvious for the user who wants to build a database from downloaded MEDLINE records. There are well over 150,000 MEDLINE records that have been truncated after the two hundred fiftieth word due to limitations of the software used in the 1960s to build the database. The size of the abstract field was extended to 400 words in the 1990s, but even that length proved to be a limit for more than 10,000 records.

Sometimes field-length limitations may be overcome by using two fields for the contents of one very long field. This is commonly done to accommodate cases where the address field is very long by offering Address-1 and Address-2 fields for street addresses and the rest of the address, respectively. Even if the maximum length of field is generously defined, such as a maximum of 4,000 characters, it may not be sufficient for full-text databases. While it is logical to split the address information into two or more fields, this is not necessarily true for other fields such as in the full text of a conference paper.

In some cases both the length of the fields and the length of the records may be limited. Designers may get away with somewhat Scroogish field length, but if most of the fields need to be used for a record, users may hit the record-length ceiling. This would not happen if the record length were very generously defined, even if it were not unlimited. AskSam, for example, has a limit of 16,000 lines per record. It is not a limit that is likely to be reached for abstracting/indexing records or even for full-text article or conference paper records. However, it still would not be able to accommodate Tolstoy's *War and Peace* as a single record. On the other hand, the limit of record length would not be a problem if the database were structured by chapters of the book.

Fixed versus Variable Field and Record Length

Another aspect of field length is the imposition of fixed fields instead of variable fields. This presents a no-win situation because for many fields the length of the attribute values varies widely from record to record. For example, a corporate name may be as simple as Aloha, Inc., and as long as Steering Committee on Leishmaniasis, UNDP/World Bank/WHO Special Programme for Research and Training in Tropical Diseases, Geneva, Switzerland. Some of the components in the name (Comm., Prog., Res., SU) may be abbreviated depending on the purpose of the database. However, a generous sizing that contemplates the longest possible value for a field will waste space for most of the records.

On the other hand, a conservatively sized field will sooner or later force the use of the truncated form of a name or title. Software without variable length field support is a Procrustean bed. This is one of the most serious limitations of mainstream database management programs that may hinder their use for textual information management systems. Such systems often have to comply with strict rules, such as online catalogs that should conform to AACR2 rules. Software packages that support variable field length typically also support variable record length.

Interdatabase Linking of Records and Fields

A possible solution for the limitations on the number of fields and size of records is offered by those programs that allow the linking of records and fields stored in different databases. This is the underlying idea behind relational database management systems, and it has been borrowed by some textual information management systems such as DB/TextWorks. (This software has no limitation on the number and length of fields; the linking feature was developed for other reasons of efficiency.)

The linking of records makes it possible, for example, to store records for conference proceedings in one database and records for individual conference papers in another. The former would include all the data related to the proceedings volume itself, and the latter the ones related to the papers themselves.

The link between the two databases is a unique identifier for each conference proceedings record. This unique identifier is then used in the conference papers database to refer to the data elements related to the proceedings volumes. In displaying and printing results the two are merged on the fly into a single virtual record. This approach can be further refined by storing the data elements related to the conference itself in a third database, such as the name, location, and sponsor of the conference, assuming that these are not likely to change often (held year after year in the same location and sponsored by the same body). This is the case, for example, with the International Online Meetings conference whose name has not changed for two decades (except for the year qualifier that would not appear in the conference record). Its location has always been London, and its sponsor has always been Learned Information, Ltd. These data elements would be invoked from the records of the fields of the proceedings volumes that describe the conference itself. The date information that varies from year to year (and the name of the editor that may change) would be stored in the records of the proceedings database.

Linking serves other purposes as well. It saves repetitive data entry, drastically reduces typos, increases consistency, and minimizes clean-up efforts. The name of the conference, for example, needs to be corrected in case of misspellings only in the conference database; the change will ripple through all the records that "loan" the conference name field when displaying or printing records either from the proceedings volume or the individual conference papers database. These benefits can be also achieved by using a substitution technique (to be described later in this chapter). However, with the linking technique, the linked content is not stored in the borrowing records as it is in the substitution technique. An added benefit is that the length of the records can be decreased to meet the record-size limitation—if any—of the software.

Database Definition

The first step in building a database is the definition of the data elements that make up the records. This critical phase in building a database requires some off-the-computer work before providing the specifications for the software. Good database design requires familiarity with the users' requirements, with the documents described by the bibliographic records, and with the capabilities of the software to be used. Consult the book of Tenopir and Lundeen.[1] Also consult Osborne and Nakamura's book for information on systems analysis.[2]

Here it is assumed that due thought was given to define the structure and content of the records and to determine the data elements needed. The record structure may be revised and modified later; however, such a decision usually implies significant changes in existing records to retrofit them to the revised structure. It is always wise to design a prototype with a few dozen records that represent the various record types and content; similarly, it is wise to test the functionality of the database with a representative group of users and possibly with one or two of the designer's peers before launching large scale data entry operations to build the database.

Sample Databases

Typically, all packages allow designers to define the content and structure of the records. Most programs also offer sample databases to help novice users in this task. The samples not only provide a sample record definition for one or more typical applications (public access catalog, acquisitions database, etc.) and record types (books, journal articles, conference papers), but they also supply the data-entry templates, the display and print formats (layouts), and—if they are separate files—the stop-word file (the terms to be ignored during indexing, such as prepositions, pronouns, etc.) and the file that specifies how the index is to be generated.

These samples are good starting points, and many users may not even need to adapt these samples. They can use them as a shell and start entering data. This out-of-the-box convenience can be appropriate for the most-routine applications, such as for a reprint collection of a re-searcher. Not accidentally, all the bibliography management software packages come with predefined database structures for dozens of document types and for hundreds of output formats.

Before using samples and templates, consider how well designed they are for the purpose. For example, although Reference Manager is particularly aimed at medical bibliographic information storage and retrieval, its journal article and book templates do not include fields for major and minor MeSH (*Medical Subject Heading*) terms, population type (male, female, human, or animal), age groups (newborn, infant, adult, etc.), language of documents, country of publication, author affiliation, or some other data elements that are common in MEDLINE databases. Although there are five user-definable fields in Reference Manager, these are not included either in the predefined output formats or in the destination fields of the capture formats specified for importing MEDLINE records. The keywords field is predefined, but it is meant for indexing words from the title and abstract fields. Putting the major and minor subject headings in the keywords field would defeat their purpose of subject authority control and the distinction by subject emphasis. Similarly, book templates have no predefined fields for Library of Congress Subject headings or for LC and Dewey classification codes—essential data elements for quality searching and for printing classified bibliographies.

Samples may have other limitations. For example, Micro-CDS/ISIS comes with a very simple sample database structure for journal articles and an even simpler one for a thesaurus. Exchanges on the ISIS-related discussion lists indicate that beginners have a difficult time defining the field-definition table, field-selection table for indexing, input worksheets, and print and display formats. The software has a steep learning curve in exchange for its powerful features. (The Windows version released in 1997 dramatically simplifies the database definition and the search formulation aspects of the software and offers an outstanding database definition wizard.) It is odd that the useful CDS/ISIS listserver does not have some sample databases from the active and genuinely cooperative members of the informal CDS/ISIS users' club. Beginning users could download such samples to help them get started. Lacking such a collection, users may only accidentally learn through postings about some remarkably good prototypes, such as the OECD (Organization for Economic Cooperation and Development) Thesaurus that is freely available.

Many of the generic database management systems also come with a few sample databases bundled. At least one of them usually can serve as a good model for a textual database. Microsoft offers a nice sample music database for music recordings in Access; FileMaker has samples for both audio and video recordings. Though these models would not have all the data elements required by an AACR2-compliant catalog, they can be immediately put to use in patron access catalogs. FileMaker Pro also has a well-designed interactive tutorial.

For an extra charge Inmagic, Inc., offers a collection of sample databases. Their design is professional, and they provide the designer of a DB/TextWorks database with an interconnected set of databases for the catalog, acquisitions file, patron and item files of the circulation system, and Kardex file of the serials control system. Inmagic's solution represents the best of both worlds because it also offers almost all the customization facilities that one can imagine. This flexibility and the impressive power features for authority control put this software ahead of the more expensive and barely customizable off-the-shelf library automation packages.

Building the Database

In some programs the database definition consists only of a listing of the data elements (fields and subfields) and their type (numeric, alphabetic, or date), length, repeatability, and authority control. In others, the definitions also include the specifications for the choice and format of indexes and at least one data-entry worksheet and one display/print format. These definitions may be treated as preliminary decisions that may be changed fairly easily. Choosing an additional field for indexing or changing the indexing mode of the author affiliation field from word indexing to phrase indexing necessitates the reindexing of the entire database. Although this can be a time-consuming process in a database of thousands of records, it is computer time intensive, not human time intensive. Changing the structure and content of records, however, has a ripple effect on all of the other decisions; therefore, their definitions should be well thought out at the beginning.

Many database-definition options can be best understood after reading chapters 6 and 10. The data entry, indexing, and output aspects of database definition will be discussed in those later chapters. The preliminary decisions for database definition must be made in a single process at the outset of building the database with a knowledge of data entry, indexing, and output requirements.

Data Entry Criteria

The quality of a database greatly depends on the power of the software that was used to create appropriate, ergonomically ideal templates for data entry and to ensure accurate and consistent data entry through the use of built-in or programmable validity checks. The other side of the coin is how competent the designers and the managers of the databases are in deploying the features of a powerful program and how committed they are to maintaining clean databases. Not even the best built-in quality checks can help if warnings are overridden and authority lists are ignored.

These same considerations apply to situations in which most of the records and data elements are imported from existing, computer-readable sources such as MARC records or when records are downloaded from a commercial database (observing the legal restrictions for the use of downloaded records). The software should be able to provide tools for checking the validity of values in certain fields, such as ISSN or ISBN; checking the presence of mandatory fields, such as the title field; and providing authoritative and consistent formats of values in fields such as descriptors, names of persons, corporations, journals, languages, author affiliations, etc. These criteria apply to both locally keyboarded records and those imported from existing sources. In fact, data entry and correction facilities are needed even if the entire database is based on imported records.

Data entry is a weak point in many textual information management programs. In contrast, many traditional database management programs offer far better quality control tools for data entry, and these traditional programs keep improving with every new release. The sorry state of many commercial databases in terms of erroneous and inconsistent data shows that search capability is a more important factor in textual information storage and retrieval software than data entry capability.

Some errors could easily be avoided and corrected even without sophisticated data entry programs if the producer has minimal quality standards. For example, it may be perceived as a sign of disrespect for the users when the language index looks like that shown in figure 5-1. The descriptor index from this producer shows a similar lack of quality.

Beyond projecting a careless and unprofessional image, erroneous and inconsistent data entries have serious implications for retrieval. In the DOS CD-ROM version of another database of this file producer, the language index is not browsable, so the users are kept in the dark about the large number of erroneous entries. As shown in figure 5-2, when searching for Portuguese language documents users will find 260 records but miss another 147 records where the language is incorrectly entered as "Portugese." In fact, until the mid-1990s there were more records with the incorrect spelling of Portuguese than with the correct spelling. Users

Figure 5-1   Excerpt from a Language Index

E23	2	LA=E GLISH
E24	1	LA=E NGLISH
E25	1	LA=EEN
E26	2	LA=EGLISH
E27	3	LA=EGNLISH
E28	2	LA=EIGLISH
E29	4	LA=EINGLISH
E30	1	LA=EMGLISH
E31	1	LA=ENBLISH
E32	5	LA=ENG
E33	1	LA=ENGIISH
E34	24	LA=ENGISH
E35	1	LA=ENGLAIH
E36	25	LA=ENGLAND
E37	1	LA=ENGLIAH
E38	2	LA=ENGLIDH
E39	2	LA=ENGLIGH
E40	1	LA-ENGLIISH
E41	1	LA=ENGLILSH

Figure 5-2   Language Index from Another Database

Ref	Items	Index-term
E2	147	LA=PORTUGESE
E3	260	*LA=PORTUGUESE
E4	1	LA=PORTUGUESE WITH ENGLISH SUMMARY
E5	1	LA=PORTUGUESE; ENGLISH SUMMARY

of the Windows version of this database are luckier because they can spot the error through a browsable language index.

Preventing and correcting such consistent errors is very simple using the global change feature to replace "Portugese" with the correctly spelled "Portuguese." This correction would have an immediate effect on the next CD-ROM edition, which is always re-created rather than just updated with new records as is done with the online version. Figure 5-3 shows a global change operation.

It is due to poor data entry software or poor management, or both, that such errors occur in the first place and remain in the database to such an extent for years. Software with good quality control features in responsible hands can contribute significantly to the value of a database.

Figure 5-3   Global Change Operation

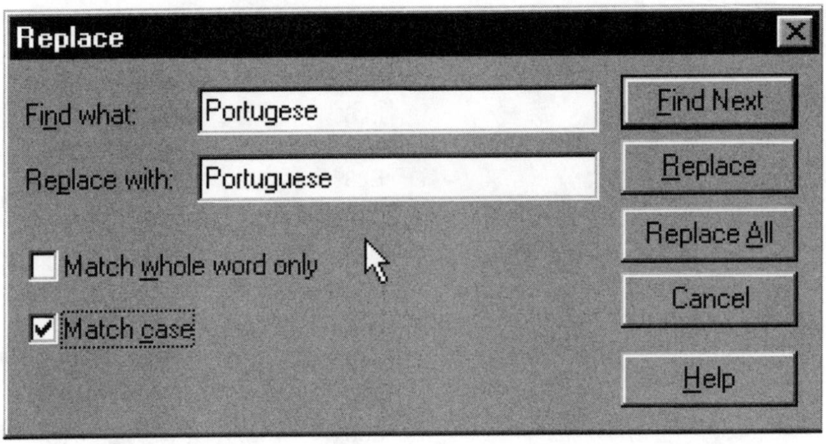

The criteria related to the data entry capabilities of the software can be grouped into those that affect template design and those that provide verification of data entry. Not all programs have all the features that are discussed here. These features may be considered as a wish list. Developers can select the most important features for them by assigning weights to these criteria (essential, desired, or useful) based on their own needs. This approach applies to all the criteria discussed.

Template Design Features

Many programs provide templates that can be helpful for the typical data entry requirements. However, because there are always special circumstances, the database designer must be able to modify these ready-to-use templates and create new ones. The following sections describe various aspects of template creation that designers may want to consider.

User-Defined Fields

When the template does not offer all the data elements needed to describe the documents as required by the user, designers must be able to create the needed fields. Many programs, such as ProCite, Reference Manager, and EndNote, offer only a few user-defined fields that may suffice for some applications but not for all.

Field Democracy

User-defined fields may be treated as second-class citizens if they cannot be indexed or cannot have authority control. This may also happen with predefined fields. For example, Reference Manager generates browsable indexes for only selected fields (author, periodical title, and keywords). Such limitations prevent the programmed use of authority files for publishers, language, country names, etc. Older versions of ProCite had similar limitations, but the latest edition offers the use of authority control files ("term lists" in ProCite's parlance) for any field. Figure 5-4 shows a portion of the term list for journal names in ProCite.

Figure 5-4   Term List for Journal Names in ProCite

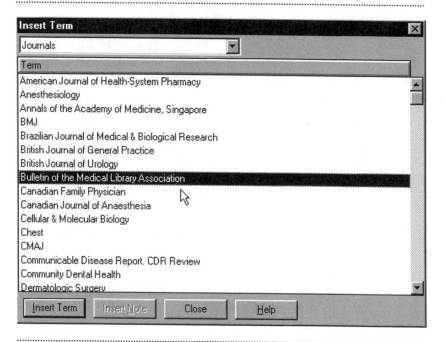

Field Rearrangement

The database designer should also be able to rearrange the data fields on the data entry template to match the sequence of the data elements as they appear on the input form, such as catalog cards or a Kardex sheet for serials check-in. This can improve the efficiency of data entry operation. The descriptive names of the fields that appear on the template should also be able to be changed by the designer. For example, the field names should be changed to Spanish for a Spanish-speaking user population.

Changeable Field Names

The overwhelming majority of software in general and textual information management software in particular is created in the United States and the United Kingdom. The programs are used, however, from Argentina to Zaire. Data entry operators feel much more comfortable if they see the field descriptions in their mother tongue or as they appear on the document surrogate used for data entry. Changing the field names was not always possible, for example, in Reference Manager, which allowed the renaming of only user-defined fields. The latest release allows users to change any of the field names. Less critical is the question if field names of multiple words are permitted or not.

Field Deletion

The ability to delete (remove) fields from a predefined template may be needed to avoid unnecessary stops in cells that are to be left empty. This is the case, for example, when there is no need for Dewey classification code in a predefined template. If unused fields cannot be deleted from a template, data entry operators may behave like bus drivers who have to pull in at a bus stop even if there are no passengers to drop off or pick up.

Template Creation

Customization may be sufficient for databases that store information about mainstream documents. Creating totally new templates is needed when there is no template to enter data for special document types, such as a database of a library's CD-ROM collection, an administrative database of minutes of board meetings, or a contract database of agreements between an agency and its consultants. The best software packages offer both customizable templates and the ability to define templates from scratch.

Automatic Record Numbering

Records must have a unique identifier in every database. The record identifier is the key element in inverted indexes. Some programs provide automatic record numbering that helps avoid the creation of duplicate record identifiers (though not duplicate records). This can be a convenience, but it should not be the only alternative; users should be allowed to create record identifiers on their own.

Multiple Templates

The software should accommodate different templates for the same record types: one for average-length records and one for long records.

This option lets the database designer optimize the screen estate for typical records and makes available an alternate template for atypical ones. The database designer should be able to define a longer template for books of a series or for translated publications, for example. The template may extend across two screens or cram more fields on a single template to accommodate such data elements as the title, ISSN, editor of the series, number within the series, or the original title of a foreign language document and its translator's name.

Unlimited Number of Fields

The usable area on the terminal screen naturally limits the number of fields and the amount of text that can be put on a single page of a template. Sometimes, however, the software defines the limit. CDS/ISIS, for example, limits to 20 the number of fields on a single screen irrespective of the length of these fields. It may happen that a quarter of the screen is empty because most of the fields are short but the total number of fields has already reached the limit.

Scrollable Field

It is a useful, though rather uncommon, feature to have scrollable fields that can be defined. This is very convenient for fields in which the length may vary enormously. In CDS/ISIS and DB/TextWorks designers may define a field on the data entry template that displays only four lines in the cell assigned for the abstract. If it is not enough for a longer abstract, the first line is automatically scrolled up to make room for the fifth line as it is being entered. Similarly, scrollable fields can be useful for fields with multiple values (repeatable fields) because the number of occurrences may vary widely. Figure 5-5 shows that the field for major descriptors (identified with the DJ field tag) is set for unlimited number of lines, and the check box next to the scroll-bar option will make the cell indicate that it is a scrollable field.

Default Values

A very important customization feature is the assignment of default field values that appear in the template whenever a new record is to be created. For example, in entering records for a branch library, its code may be made a default value along with the predominant field values such as language (for example, English), country of publication (United States), etc. Default values need to be overwritten by the operator only if the language is not English and the country of publication is not the United States. A variation of this option is when some of the field values may be

Figure 5-5   Scrollable Field Definition in DB/TextWorks

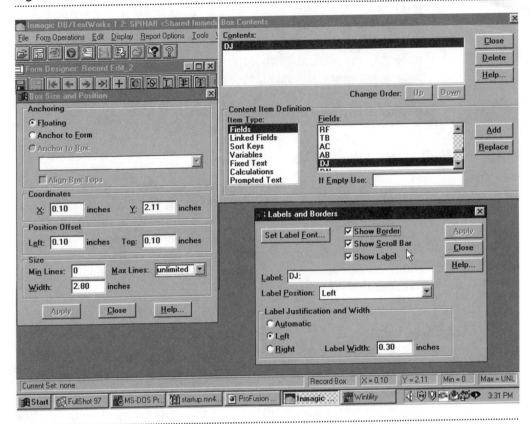

automatically supplied by the system, such as the date and time for entering/updating the record. Date and time don't need to be displayed on the template, but they must be specified during database definition.

To save space, the common practice is to use short field tags as shown in figure 5-6 instead of spelled out ones. Data entry operators would have instructions on what to enter in the cells, listing the acronyms, such as RI for Record Identifier, PI for the Page Image file name, TI for Title, ST for Subtitle, and so on. They may be using input forms that already have these field tags. Users would figure out that SP is the Start Page, EP is the End Page, TP is the Total Page, and a help file listing all the field tags would help them out if needed. Some programs allow the designer to create an alternative template with long field names both for data entry and for searching.

Figure 5-6   Default Values in a Template in DB/TextWorks

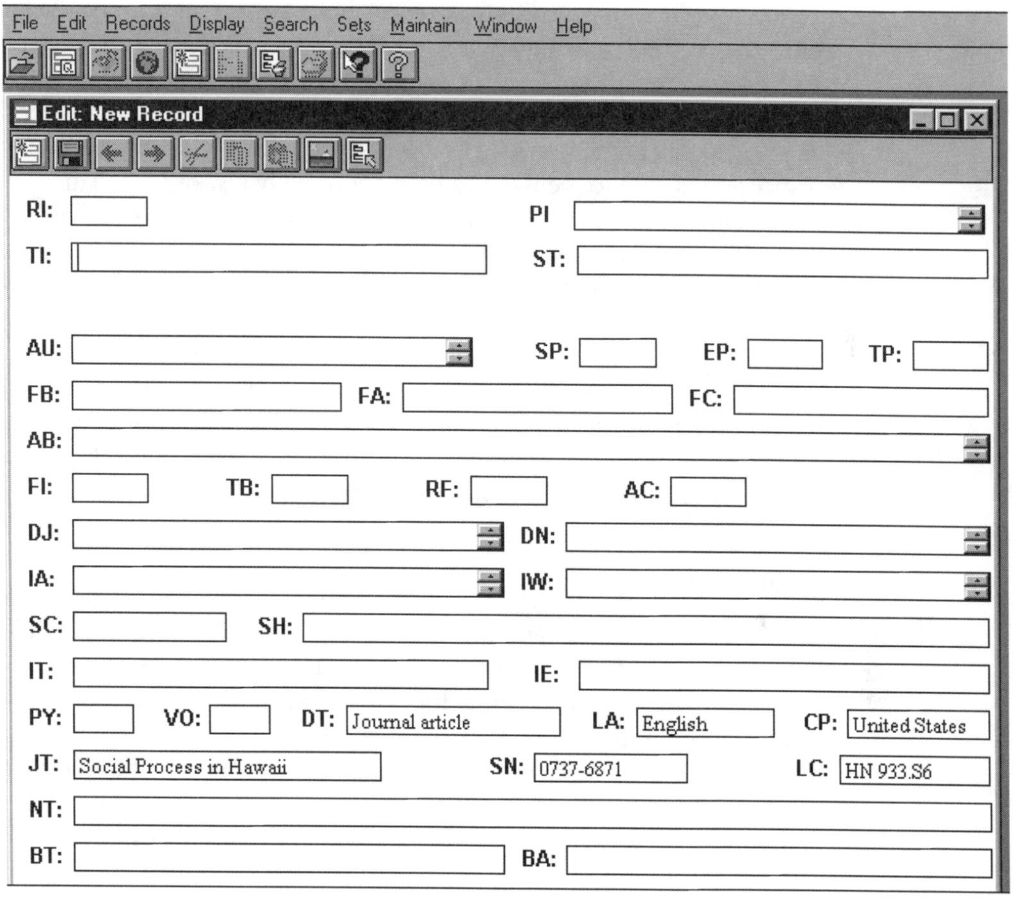

Spawned Fields

Spawning fields is a convenient way for repeating the same value from record to record without making the content a default value for all of the records. Spawning is not a widely used term; FileMaker Pro refers to it as "selecting value from previous record." For example, entering a series of records for each chapter in a book could be accelerated if common elements (title, editor, ISBN, publisher, etc.) could be brought forward from one record to another. This is particularly useful if the software does not support linked files to borrow data elements.

Computed and Generated Field Values

Fields may be computed automatically from two or more other fields after they are entered. For example, the product of the unit price ($5) and the number of copies ordered (4) could be used to automatically compute and create the entry in the value of the order field ($20) as soon as the contents of the previous two fields are typed in. The operator may glance at this field to see if the value is abnormally low or high. This may happen if, for example, 22 copies are entered accidentally instead of 2 or if a $.75 unit price is used instead of $75.

Similar is the generated field values feature that would trigger the automatic display of a code or text when entering a field value. For example, filling out the first and last year of publication for a serials record will generate the value of the serials status field as "ceased" unless the value entered in the last year of publication is "9999." This is a special value in cataloging practice that indicates an active status. This value should in turn trigger the generation of the entry "active" for the status field.

Copying Authority List Terms

For the sake of accuracy and consistency there should be an authority file for as many data elements as possible in a database. These may be local authority files, such as the authority list of department names in a course catalog database of a university. If such authority lists can be popped up during data entry and items can be pasted from the list into the record, it improves accuracy and consistency significantly. Figure 5-7 shows an authority list from which terms can be pasted in the record being edited.

Field-Value Substitution

Substituted field values facilitate data entry and ensure consistency. The data entry operator has to enter only a code, such as UHM, and the software—using a substitution file, also known as a *look-up file*—will substitute the code with the spelled-out format: University of Hawaii at Manoa. UHH would be substituted by University of Hawaii at Hilo. Figure 5-8 shows substitution values for the three-character library codes in a union catalog.

Field substitution also offers another advantage. Changes must be made only in this look-up file, not in the records themselves. For example, if the address of the serials jobber has changed, it needs to be corrected only in the substitution file, and the new address will appear in all the order records that use the code or abbreviation for that substitution.

Figure 5-7   Authority List with Terms That Can Be Pasted in DB/TextWorks

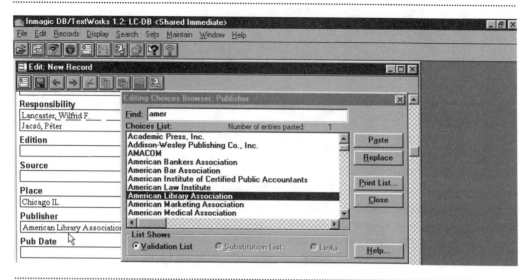

Figure 5-8   Substitution File in DB/TextWorks

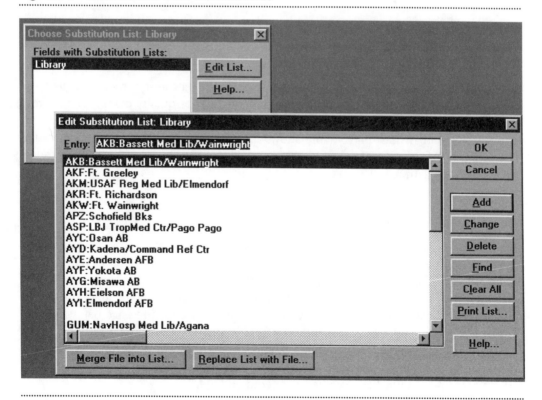

Some software may limit the use of substitute terms to certain fields; in ProCite their use (known as *alternate text*) is limited to the printed output and is not shown on the screen.

Most programs allow the creation of substitute lists off-line. This is a great convenience, especially when the substitute list is available in computer-readable format. The synonym list in Reference Manager cannot be created and edited off-line.

Color Coding of Template Cells

Entering records is a monotonous task. Good graphic design that guides the operator is a trait of the best software. Customization extends also to the graphic design of the template. For example, cells with different colors may indicate mandatory versus required-if-available field types. Beyond visual aids to support quality data entry, the software should also have features to check the validity of the data entered.

Verification Features

Good template design can help make the data entry process efficient and of high quality, but the ultimate tool set for quality control comes from the verification features of the program. These can reduce most of the errors that unavoidably show up in any data-entry process. Verification features serve purposes similar to those of copy editors and proofreaders with manuscripts.

Mandatory-Field Check

The most essential control that the software should provide is the check for the presence of mandatory fields. The title field in a bibliographic database or corporate name in the vendor file of an acquisition system must be present in every record. The software must offer an option to declare such fields mandatory and check for their presence before accepting a record. If a mandatory field is missing, a warning should be issued to the data entry operator about the condition. For example, as shown in figure 5-9, because no record should appear without a title field, the title field must be specified as a required field.

Figure 5-9 Specifying Required Fields in DB/TextWorks

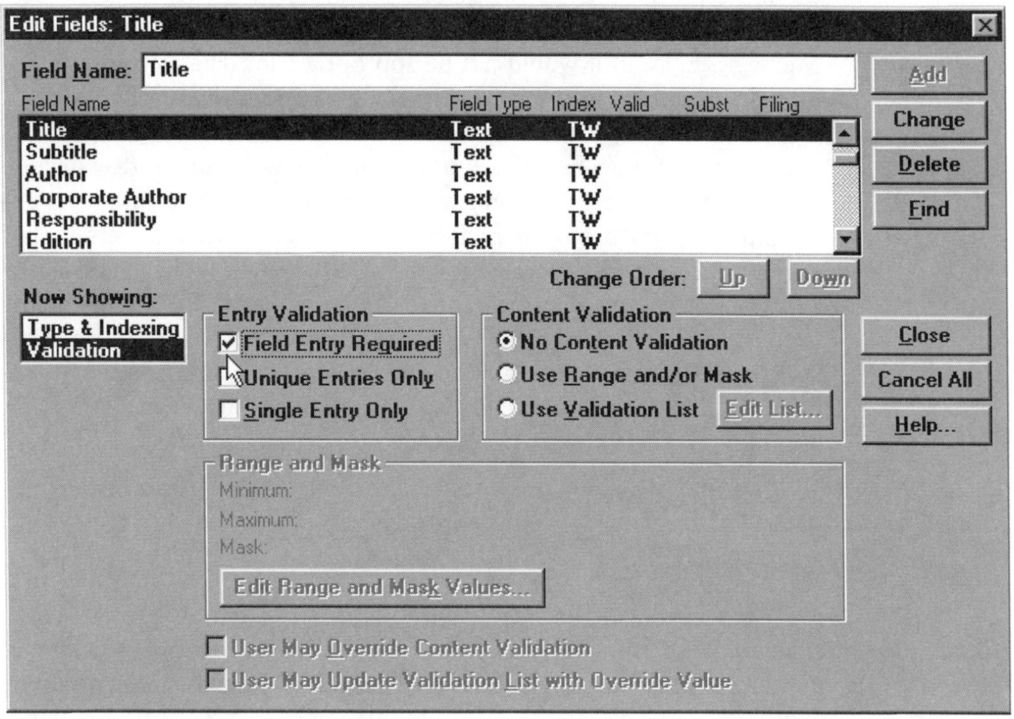

Beyond the mere presence of a field, the software should be able to check the content of fields. The extent of validity checking of field values varies from data element to data element and from database to database. Clear error messages help the operators spot the error. Another useful option allows the designer to specify that the operator can override the validity check. Of course, this can be abused by data entry personnel, but it is a management issue to prevent such abuse. The following are the basic common data-entry features that check the content of the fields.

Field-Type Check

In defining the record structure, data fields are typically classified into a specific category, such as alphanumeric, purely numeric, alphabetic, or date field. The software would automatically check if the field includes only numbers or only alpha characters. The more categories there are, the more powerful the error detection can be. A strictly numeric field may be appropriate for a field such as the number of copies in an acquisitions system, but it would not be appropriate for data elements that—though considered numbers—include alphabetic and special characters.

Despite its name, the International Standard Book Number (ISBN) is not a number from a field definition point of view because it may include the letter X in the last position and, depending on the data entry convention, may include one or more hyphens. Fax and phone numbers are not numeric fields either, because of the parentheses, hyphen, and space characters. The publisher name field may seem to be alphabetic, but in reality it may include a hyphen or a slash as part of the name, as in Neal-Schuman. Defining such fields as alphanumeric to accept numbers, alphabetic, and special characters would reduce quality control errors by type of field. The software should offer other means to check the content of the field.

Unique-Field Value

Every record in a database must have one field with a unique value that distinguishes it from other records and provides an unambiguous identification. It could be a sequence number, an ID (such as an employee number), or a code built from a combination of different data elements. The software should offer the option of designating one or more fields that must have a unique value and check for its uniqueness against the other records in the database.

Duplicate Detection

Even though the records may have a unique identifier, more than one record for the same entity might appear in a database. For example, a journal may be covered by more than one abstractor, records may have been imported from external sources, or data entry operators may have accidentally created two records from the same work sheet.

An increasing number of programs offer duplicate detection, and some offer it with a user-controlled level of strictness. Reference Manager, for example, can search for duplicates looking for an exact, letter-by-letter match in certain fields such as author, title, journal name, publication year, but it also offers the option of detecting duplicates by loosening the criteria. For example, the more lenient alternative would identify as duplicates two records in which the authors' middle names or the subtitles don't match but the rest of the compared data elements do. Although EndNote does not offer the option to customize the duplicate detection algorithm, it smartly checks the last name and the first initials of the authors (along with the title, year, and document type fields). It is a more appropriate option than the last-name-only versus full-name choice in Reference Manager (as shown in figure 5-10).

Duplicates may be real or phantom. For example, a generic title may be used for the regular column of an author (such as *Péter's Picks & Pans*), and only the volume and issue number together may be the distinguishing factors that reveal that these are not duplicates. At least if the

Figure 5-10   Duplicate Detection Algorithms in Reference Manager

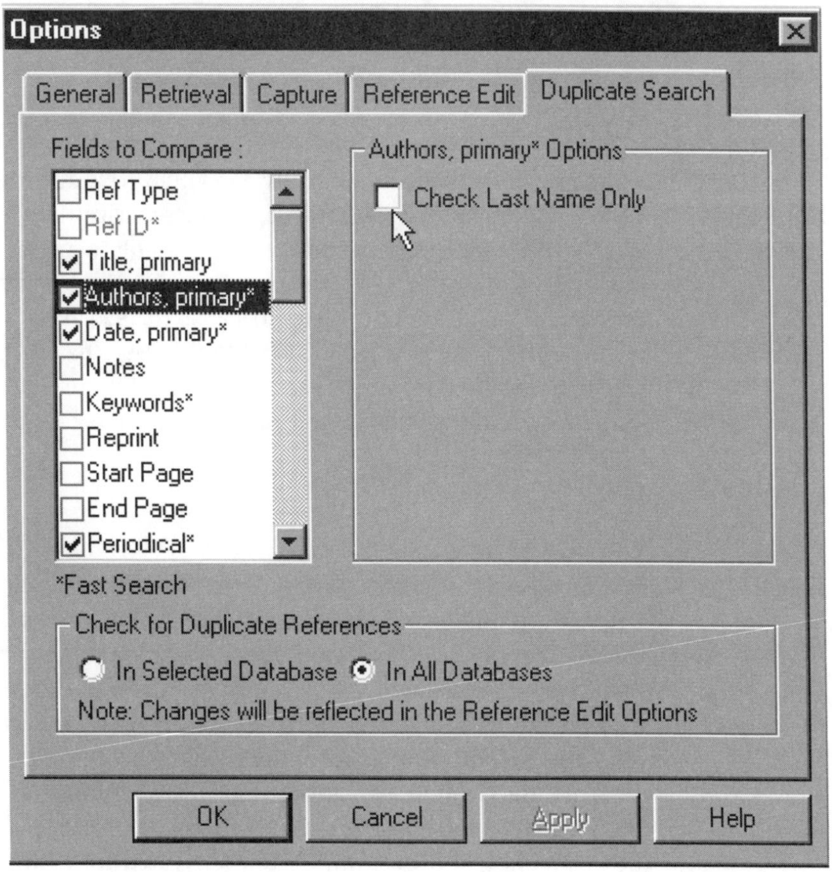

software offers duplicate detection at varying degrees of strictness, the person responsible for quality control could look at the duplicate list to decide if the records are genuine duplicates. Intelligent duplicate detection features can prevent an excessive number of duplicates from getting into a database.

Field-Length Check

Automatically checking the length of a field is a common feature. For fields of predictable length, the data entry cell itself may be a guide that prevents the data entry operator from entering a value longer than the space provided. For example, a three-character position for a library branch code would not allow the accidental entry of a four-character code. However, this still would not prevent an operator from entering a two-character code unless the required length of the field value can be specified as three characters, and the software checks that it is neither longer nor shorter.

Pattern Check

For some data elements not only the length but also the pattern of the data is predictable. For example, social security numbers should have the 999-99-9999 pattern, where 9 represents a numeric value. Obviously, the software used to issue a Hawaii state identification card does not have a pattern check feature because the social security number appears in the following pattern: 999999-9999, that is, the first hyphen was replaced by a number that it made up. Figure 5-11 shows the pattern check options of Microsoft Access that refers to it as an input mask.

Range Check

The software should offer a range check to verify if a field value is within a minimum and maximum range. This is also known as a plausibility check. For example, the publication year field for printed materials should have a reasonable range check from 1400 to the current year. For an acquisitions system the upper limit, of course, could be extended beyond the current year to accommodate forthcoming books. This could prevent a publication year appearing as 1097 instead of 1997, for example. Figure 5-12 shows the editing of range values of publication year in the abstracting and indexing database created for a single journal pub-

Figure 5-11   Pattern Check Feature in Microsoft Access

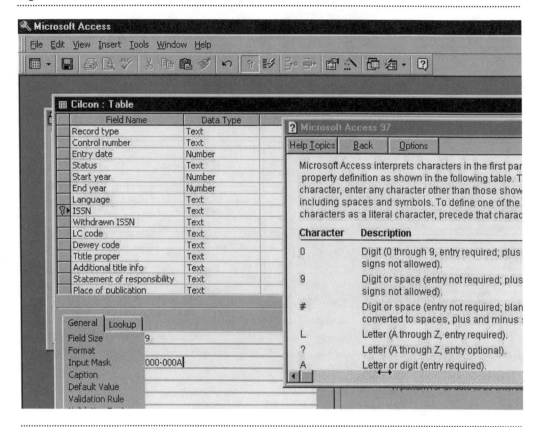

lished first in 1937. Obviously, the upper limit has to be changed every year after 1998.

Check-Digit Validation

It is ironic that none of the commercial library programs now available offer check-digit validation to prevent invalid ISBNs and ISSNs in a database. The last digit of each number is calculated from the other digits via a simple algorithm. The check-digit concept was devised exactly for programmed control; it is not for human checking.

The data entry programs specifically meant for creating databases for library materials should have a built-in function to recalculate and validate the check digit of the ISSN and ISBN numbers entered. The authors of a set of custom-made utility programs (OSIRIS for Micro-CDS/ISIS)

Figure 5-12   Range Check Feature in DB/TextWorks

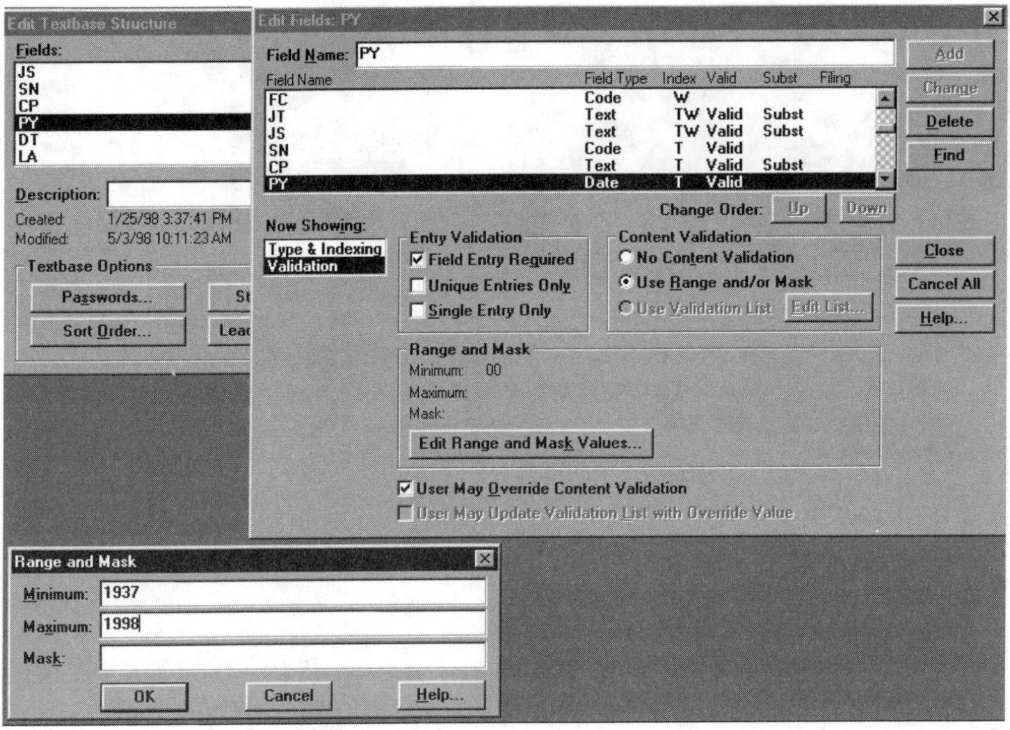

implemented such a check-digit validation algorithm as shown in figure 5-13. The program tests the validity of the check digit either for ISSNs entered from the keyboard or from a file and helps spot typos in these essential control numbers for serials.

Validation Lists (Authority Files)

Sometimes none of the previously mentioned checks can prevent an erroneous entry. State codes, country codes, and language codes range from A to Z; Standard Industry Classification Codes cover a broad range that cannot be verified by any of the automated checking methods. However, the values of such fields can be effectively controlled if the software offers validation lists, or authority files, against which the data entered are compared.

The software should allow the designer to create and maintain a list of valid values that the software would use as an authority file. Though some of these lists may consist of thousands of possible values, many of

Figure 5-13 Check-Digit Validation of ISSN in OSIRIS

them are available in computer-readable format and could be transferred to the software as the authority file. State codes (abbreviations), language codes, country codes, SIC (Standard Industry Classification) codes belong to this category. Most of them are available from the Web sites of the agencies responsible for their maintenance, the Library of Congress, and the U.S. Commerce Department. For example, the registrar's office may make available the list of valid social security numbers of faculty, staff, and students for creating the patron file for a circulation database in an academic library. Lists of valid descriptors, section headings, and classification codes could be extracted from existing files and used as authority lists. For example, valid U.S. state codes could be easily entered from scratch into an authority file. A list of country codes used by the International Standards Organization, the Library of Congress, or the United Nations could be easily obtained and converted into authority files.

In some large-scale operations, authority files indeed have been used, but the files are often limited to the personal author name, corporate name, and descriptor fields. Thousands of databases bear witness to the fact that journal names, series names, country names, language names, SIC codes, and SIC names are not under any kind of authority control. Sometimes even the descriptor field—the prime example for using controlled vocabulary—evades checking against an authority file.

Validation Override

For some fields the data entry operator should have the option of overriding the validity control after receiving a warning. For example, forthcoming books may have a publication year later than 2000 instead of 1999. Also, if the exact year of publication is unknown, the value may be less than 1400 or more than 2000 because the computer will reject 199? or 1??? as being outside the specified range. The override option could be applicable for other types of checks as well. The (sub)fields for invalid and withdrawn ISSNs should also be able to accommodate ISSN values in the wrong pattern, of the wrong length, or with an invalid check digit.

Importing Records

Instead of creating records from scratch, it is much more efficient to import records in computer-readable formats. Though this process is less than perfect, it keeps improving and is worth learning about for anyone who wants to create a database for documents (books, journal articles, conference papers, or dissertations) other than in-house memos and documents of only local relevance. Importing records has a long history in the mainframe world; it is worth recapping here to better understand the concept. There are also numerous import/export formats, also known as exchange formats. Instead of trying to explain the differences of the various formats, appendix B shows a series of records for the same book in various import and export formats. These import formats are not for reading by the naked eye. They are read by the import module of the program. The designer may need to look at some of the records in import format if there is an error in the process. The user documentation explains the syntax of the import formats in detail or refers the designer to national and international standards. Tags and special symbols identify the beginning and ending of records, fields, and—if applicable—subfields. End-users don't need to deal with this format.

Historical Milestones

For decades the importing of records to build a local database has been common practice for online catalogs based on mainframe computer systems. Bibliographic information management programs used on main-frame systems have been able to import records in the MARC Communications format. The millions of records created by the Library of Congress and member libraries of the various bibliographic utilities (OCLC, RLIN, WLN) have been imported to create the online public access catalogs of academic libraries and major public and special libraries since the 1960s. Based on the success of the distribution of MARC records, national libraries around the world embarked on similar projects from the 1970s. This spawned a variety of MARC formats (USMARC, UK-MARC, CANMARC, HUNMARC, and SINMARC) that followed the same concept but differed slightly in implementation. International agencies also started to distribute their databases so customers could select and download records for creating their own subsets.

Hindrances

The introduction of microcomputers could not immediately benefit from these efforts because the records were distributed on nine-inch tapes, and personal computers typically did not have tape drives. The tape drives that were on the market for PCs were selling at mainframe prices, costing more than the PCs. CD-ROMs brought a change in the scene in the mid-1980s, and one of the first CD-ROM applications, Bibliofile, from The Library Corporation, was targeted for customers who wanted to create local catalogs from MARC records on their PCs. This was a breakthrough product that inspired numerous other CD-ROM databases that could provide records in MARC format both in the United States and abroad.

Parallel to the proliferation of microcomputers in information work, users realized the advantage of downloading records to their hard drives and studying the results off-line. This was a necessary step because online information services were charging fees based on connect time. Though connect time charges did not apply to the CD-ROM abstracting and indexing databases, downloading records from CD-ROM sources became an issue, too. Users could not always print the results from these sources that were accessed through public access PCs that did not have a printer attached or that had a worn-out ink-jet printer attached that was used for many workstations at the same time.

The next logical steps were to store the results of online searches not only as plain text files but also as uploaded records in local, personal databases. The uploaded records provided for flexible, easy retrieval without the need of searching the online or CD-ROM database again. Both developments were hindered by the lack of appropriate software on the PCs and the Macs for importing records in MARC format. The variety of inconsistent and often-changing formats used by the different online and CD-ROM information providers and the file producers aggravated the situation.

Stand-Alone and Integrated Converters

Developers of bibliographic information management software offered—
for a rather steep extra charge—utility programs that were supposed to
convert records downloaded from some databases of some online or CD-
ROM publishers into the format that the host software could import. Personal Bibliographic Software's Bibliolink, Research Information Systems'
Capture, and Niles Software's EndLink were offered for ProCite, Reference
Manager, and EndNote, respectively. None of them worked appropriately
except for a few of the databases. Part of the reason for the surprising in-
adequacy of these converter programs was the ever-changing format of
the records downloaded from online and CD-ROM databases. The developers later offered editing possibilities for the filters of their conversion
programs. That helped some users cope with the problems, but it was not
the out-of-the-box solution that many users expected.

By 1998 all the above software developers integrated the conversion
programs into their own products (ProCite, Reference Manager, and
EndNote) without extra charge. For example, EndNote chose the most
sophisticated option. That is, users search online databases directly from
EndNote and store the results directly into an existing or new EndNote
database. This elegant solution makes downloading and importing totally transparent. In spite of these developments, conversion glitches remain. For example, hundreds of messages have been sent by users to the
discussion list of Reference Manager about conversion problems. This
list is very responsive and often provides helpful advice to users.

Third-Party Conversion Programs

A few independent software developers recognized the need for powerful conversion tools or developed one for their own purposes and made
it available free of charge. The most powerful conversion tool, Data Magician from Folland Software Services, can convert records to and from
the proprietary formats of dBASE, Inmagic, DB/TextWorks, and Library
Master as well as the standard delimited, tagged, and MARC Communications format (including its variant used by Micro-CDS/ISIS). Despite
its very sophisticated repertoire of conversion instructions (a mini programming language in itself), its $250 price tag is less than Bibliolink,
Capture, and EndLink used to cost. Data Magician can break fields into
subfields, combine and rearrange them based on complex conditions,
and substitute values through look-up tables (for example, to replace
country codes with fully spelled out versions).

MARC RTP, from Australian software developers Ross Johnson and
Lynette Taylor, is a useful $200 program for those who want to convert
records in MARC Communications format into tab-delimited and
comma-delimited formats. (These are the export/import formats sup-

ported by almost all generic database management and spreadsheet programs as well as by bibliographic information management programs.) In addition, it can create a labeled version of records in MARC Communications format and provide statistics about the fields in a collection of MARC records.

Among the freeware conversion programs, that of Fangorn stands out. Developed by two experienced Micro-CDS/ISIS programmers, Hugo Besemer and Paul Nieuwenhuysen, the program can convert tagged records downloaded from CD-ROM and online databases into the MARC variant used by Micro-CDS/ISIS. Although its capabilities do not come close to those of Data Magician, it deftly handles subfields and repeatable fields as well as replacement strings.

BookWhere 2000, from Sea Change Corporation, is primarily a client program that runs on the user's computer to establish communication with and search databases that comply with the Z39.50 standard. (This standard regulates the protocols that allow searching of this database using a uniform language.) It does that job very well and on the side provides an outstanding conversion service by converting the records retrieved into MARC Communications, comma-delimited, and tab-delimited formats as well as into the input formats used by Inmagic (DB/TextWorks), Reference Manager, ProCite, and a couple of other formats. Although some problems were found in the conversion into Reference Manager's input format, the other conversions were perfect. Considering the double functionality of this program (a search client and a polyglot conversion program), the list price of $250 makes it a bargain.

Correcting Legacy Data

Ergonomic design of input worksheets and powerful data-entry validation features can reduce erroneous data significantly while data are being entered. Legacy databases that go back 25 to 30 years pose a special problem. Data entry programs were very rudimentary in the 1960s, and erroneous records could easily make it to the database. They haunt current searchers if they need access to records from an old section of such a database. Large scale retrospective correction of errors can be quite expensive, but many errors could be eliminated very easily using global change operations supported by the database management or textual information management software or by an independent program.

The more sophisticated versions of global change operations allow the replacement of character strings, words, and terms in specific (sub)fields, even in specific occurrences of (sub)fields. This feature may be needed when the second and third authors' names should be preceded or followed by a special character to treat them as separate occurrences for proper indexing or sorting. Global change should allow field-specific changes across the entire database or selected subsets of records. For example, if coauthors used to be entered as a single field in the database such as AU: Lancaster, F. W. and Jacsó, P., software with decent global-change features may easily change the space-and-space string to a % character—the symbol of a repeatable field—in the author field (but not in the statement of responsibility field) such as AU: Lancaster, F. W.%Jacsó, P.

This simple change can have an impact on different functions of the database. The original format may have generated a single entry in the author index, such as AU=LANCASTER, F. W. AND JACSO, P. Searching by AU=JACSO, ? would not retrieve this entry. The recommended change also generates an index entry for the second author for searching; that is, there is an entry for AU=LANCASTER, F. W. and another for AU=JACSO, P. Additionally, a full record can be printed under the name of both the first and the second author in a bibliography sorted by author. A powerful program could also offer the option of printing only a *see* reference to the entry under the name of the second author if that is the convention in the bibliography.

The MARC Review software from the MARC of Quality, Inc., is a unique program that analyzes MARC records to detect and warn the data entry operator or the quality controller of certain types of erroneous entries, obsolete codes, incorrect filing indicators, missing subject headings for nonfiction books, etc. MARC Global does the correction automatically and keeps a log of the changes made.

Clean, consistent, accurate, and nonredundant data are the prerequisites for a high quality database. Sloppy data entry and many duplicate records give a bad impression of a database's quality. These are not academic problems but practical ones that may have professional and financial impacts on the users. For example, if a searcher does not find almost half of the record when limiting the search to a specific journal name because there are two or three spelling variations of it, the results would be very misleading. Duplicate and triplicate records may not only distort the results, and the conclusions in case of a bibliometric or scientometric search, but they make users pay twice for the practically identical records that show up in a search. At $1 and more per record, these extras can quickly add up in an often-searched database.

Notes   1. Carol Tenopir and Gerald Lundeen, *Managing Your Information: How to Design and Create a Textual Database on Your Microcomputer* (New York: Neal-Schuman, 1988).

2. Larry N. Osborne and Margaret Nakamura, *Systems Analysis for Librarians and Information Professionals* (Englewood, Colo.: Libraries Unlimited, 1998).

6

Index Creation

Fast and precise access to records in a database is determined by the variety of indexes created from the data elements and by the search features of the software. The two are complementary. Sophisticated index creation features are provided by the software only if the retrieval module can make use of the index entries generated. The most powerful search features can be used only if the appropriate index entries were created.

The term *indexing* is used synonymously with *index creation* in Part II of this book. Either term refers to the features associated with the automatic extraction by the program of words and terms from the records to build an index for retrieval. Indexing a database is different from the intellectual document subject indexing process in which humans assign index terms to a document to describe its characteristics, as discussed in chapter 3.

Index creation capabilities also depend on the structuring of the records. The more granular the structure of a record is, the more versatile the index creation process can be. Even software with the best index creation capabilities cannot help if, for example, authors' last names, first names, middle initials, and the names of their affiliations are lumped into one unstructured field. Similarly, if all the elements of an address (street number, street name, city, state, and ZIP code) are put into one field, the indexing program may not be able to extract correctly the name of the city or the state from this field. The smartest conversion programs are capable of recognizing some of the patterns in some of the fields and can disassemble them into their elements. For example, it is possible to break the address field into its components by recognizing the beginning and/or end of the components, such as a comma before the state or a five-digit number to indicate ZIP code, but such re-creations are never perfect. For example, the five-digit number may be part of a street address, the ZIP code may be nine digits separated by a hyphen, the state may be spelled out or abbreviated, or the database may need to accommodate Canadian addresses with their different ZIP code structure. What humans—looking at the entire context—can easily recognize as the name of the city in an address, the program may fail to identify even if the programmer thought of a large number of possible variations.

Deep structuring of records is a prerequisite for versatile indexing, and a commitment needs to be made at the database design stage. It is possible that the database designer does not want to make use of all the index creation features at the beginning of a database building process but later would like to create a more complex index. If the elements of the records are appropriately structured, index re-creation is a fairly easy process. Reindexing may be quite time-consuming, but it involves computer time and not human time.

Choice of Data Elements for Indexing

The software should offer unlimited choice for selecting the indexable data elements. Many software packages limit the number of fields to be indexed. If the limit is high, such as fifty fields, it is not a problem, but low limits of six to eight fields often may be too restrictive.

Field Indexing

Limits on indexable fields are extremely constraining when the software defines what fields can be indexed. This is the case, for example, with Reference Manager, which creates an index only for the author, journal name, reference ID, reference type, publication year, reprint status, and keyword fields (that may include words from the title and note field). However, the publisher field and the user-defined fields cannot be indexed, and that's quite a serious limitation. On the other hand, in Micro-CDS/ISIS, DB/TextWorks, and even in EndNote, which belongs to the same league of programs as Reference Manager, the designer can select any of the fields for indexing. (See figure 6-1.)

Subfield Indexing

Few programs support subfields, and even fewer support subfield indexing. This may force the designer to assign separate fields to the data elements that are traditionally treated as subfields within a single field. For

Figure 6-1 **Selecting a Field for Indexing in EndNote**

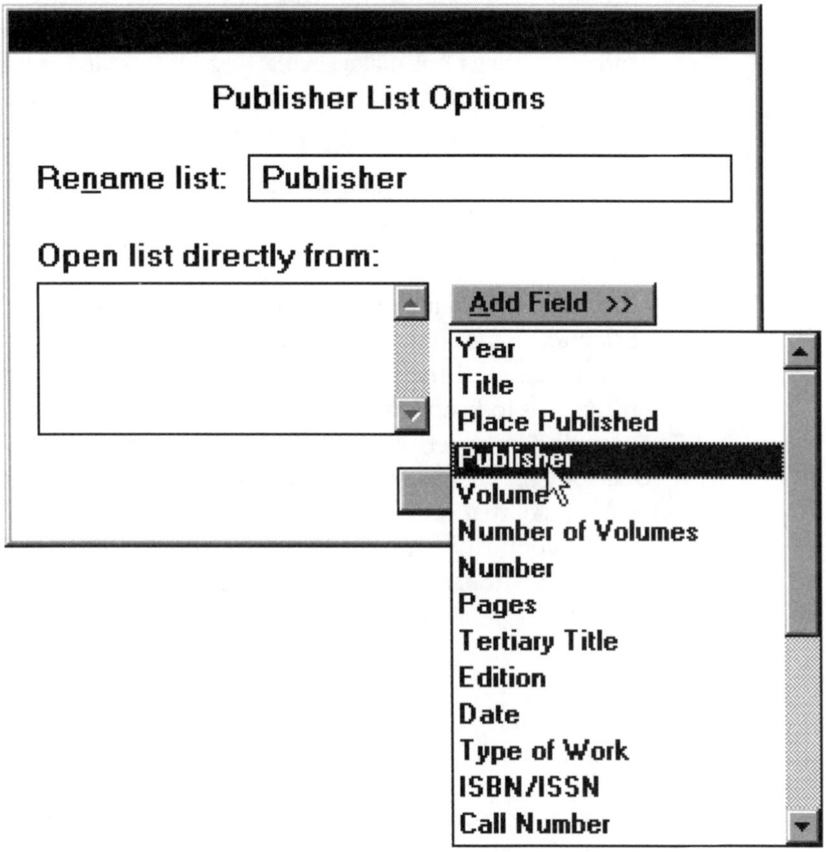

....

Publisher List Options

Re<u>n</u>ame list: | Publisher |

Open list directly from:

| | | <u>A</u>dd Field >> |

Year
Title
Place Published
Publisher
Volume
Number of Volumes
Number
Pages
Tertiary Title
Edition
Date
Type of Work
ISBN/ISSN
Call Number

....

example, in the formatted contents note of the MARC record of a collective work, subfield $a is used for the titles of the individual works and subfield $r for the related statement of responsibility (assuming that $ is the subfield delimiter). If indexes need to be created for both the titles and the authors of the individual works but the software does not offer subfield extraction for index creation, the names of the authors should be placed in a separate field from the titles in the content notes. This in turn may cause problems in matching author fields with the title fields when displaying or printing the records, especially when multiple authors are to be linked with the same title.

In another example, indexing the series title subfield of the series statement field ($aDatabase Searching Series$xNo. 4) without the volume number subfield is desired for a fine catalog. If no subfield indexing is possible, a separate field must be created for the volume number. The compromise is to index the series statement field as a whole. However, this will create as many entries in the index for the series as there are volumes having a record in the database. This increases the size of the index and does not make the catalog look professional. For example, if there are records about three volumes in the catalog, there would be three entries:

> SE=Database Searching Series, no.1
> SE=Database Searching Series, no. 2
> SE=Database Searching Series, no. 3

Instead of the single entry expected in the series index for Database Searching Series, there are three entries. In a large collection the collocation function of the index is lost because the entries get scattered. The patron has to keep scrolling in the index to get from series to series when browsing. A better practice is to have a single entry for each series title. Clicking on a series title would, in turn, display the short entry list of the volumes of that series held by the library.

In contrast, software that offers subfield indexing, such as Micro-CDS/ISIS, simply needs the following instruction to create an index from subfield ^a, as shown below

> 0 mhu, "SE=",v499$a/,,

This statement instructs the program to extract the title subfield ($a) from the series field (v499), precede it with a prefix (SE=), and create a phrase index (the 0 mhu part of the statement).

Micro-CDS/ISIS may be the only software that allows subfield indexing and offers the opportunity to specify which occurrence of a field or subfield should be indexed. This is very handy, for example, when only the first occurrence of the publisher name subfield but all occurrences of the author subfield of the formatted contents note field must be indexed.

Substring Indexing

Substring indexing, another unique feature of Micro-CDS/ISIS, may seem as if it is an esoteric feature, but it is not. Anyone who ever looked at a MARC record would know that the 008 field includes a number of data elements, including the control number of the record, the date of entry, language and country code of publication, etc., that are often needed for searching and are, therefore, prime candidates for indexing. Some of the data elements may also appear in specific fields of the record (such as the frequency of issue of a serial), but many others appear only in the 008 field. This is one of the very few fixed-length fields in MARC. The various data elements in this field are identified by their exact position within the field, not by subfield codes and subfield identifiers or by punctuation symbols. Substring indexing makes it possible, for example, to extract the code of the country of publication (and, for certain countries, the state or province of the place of publication), the language code, the status code, the frequency code, and the first and last year of publication of serials records. This is done by simply specifying the displacement of the field from the beginning of the record and the length of the substring.

Substring indexing can be very handy also for such simple fields as the date of publication. If the format of this field is dd-mm-yyyy, indexing it does not make much sense unless dates are searched by the day of the month, an unlikely event except for birthday-searching trivia. On the other hand, a year index can be easily created by specifying that the content of this field from the seventh position should be indexed as four characters. Following is the indexing statement for such a substring extraction in Micro-CDS/ISIS:

0 mhu, "PY=",v350*7(4)/

This statement instructs the program to extract four characters starting at the seventh position in Field 350 and to add a PY= prefix in creating the publication year index. The same result can be achieved by adding an extra field for just the publication year, but it is easy to run out of fields with some programs that limit the number of fields. When using an existing data source imported from another database, it is an error-prone and slow process to go through all the records manually and to enter the last four characters of the date year (dd-mm-yyyy) into the publication year field (yyyy). This indexing facility is even more desirable in a system that uses highly structured, fixed-length identifiers for documents, persons, and companies where, for example, the fifth position in an ID number may indicate if the person is a faculty member, student, or staff member and the sixth position stands for the gender code. Substring indexing makes it easy to extract and generate the appropriate index terms.

Marked-String Indexing

Marked-string indexing is the least used choice for index term selection because a human must read the text and mark the strings that should be extracted for indexing. Another reason for its obscurity is that it is not really needed in languages that use prepositions with a noun (such as English, French, German, Spanish, Italian). However, some languages use suffixes in place of prepositions. For example, the Hungarian equivalents of *in Honolulu, from Honolulu,* and *about Honolulu* are *Honolulu*ban, *Honolulu*ból, *Honolulu*ról.

Using a stop-word list for prepositions creates a clean list of terms in the English, French, German, Spanish, or Italian language databases. In the Hungarian language database, including prepositions on the stop-word list cannot help because suffixes are used and all the suffixed versions will appear in the index. Entries with different suffix variants of the same basic term would create a rather messy index.

In indexing a Hungarian-language database in the mid-1970s, marked-string indexing had to be used for the title and abstract fields to provide enhanced subject access. Keywords then were identified in those two fields and marked with a pair of triangular brackets to retain only the root of the words for the index. For example, <Honolulu>ban, <Honolulu>ból, <Honolulu>ról. This choice of data element for indexing was a compromise; it was time consuming to do the marking and unappealing to read the text, but at that time there was no other choice for enhanced subject access from the abstract.

Modes of Indexing

There are two basic modes of indexing: word indexing and term indexing. The latter is also known as phrase indexing. Many software packages only offer one mode, not both. The best software products offer both word and term indexing both with and without prefixes. Additional indexing modes are rare.

Word Indexing

Word indexing may seem to be rather straightforward. The software creates an index entry for every word in a field or subfield except for those words that are on a stop-word or skip-word list. *Skip word* is the better term because indexing does not stop on encountering one of those words in the (sub)field that are not to be indexed, such as articles, prepositions, or conjunctions; these words are merely skipped. However, *stop word* is the most widely accepted term for this feature.

What is a word for the human eye is not necessarily a word for the software. Hawai'i spelled in the authentic form with the glottal stop symbol becomes two "words" for many indexing program: *Hawai* and *i*. The same is true for names and words with an apostrophe (Alzheimer's), a hyphen (CD-ROM), one or more periods (I.B.M. [probably used only by the *New York Times* and Bowker]), a slash (AC/DC), or an ampersand (AT&T). Again, the most-intelligent programs, such as CDS/ISIS (in all of its mainframe, mini, and micro versions), offer the designer a parameter list to specify which characters should be interpreted as word separators. Personal experience taught this consideration in a bitter way when the stop-word list was not modified; consequently, numbers acted as word separators: All formula names were split, and all their components became a "word." Instead of H2SO4 there were entries for H, 2, SO, and 4. (The chemical formula should read H_2SO_4 of course, but most computer files do not use subscripts or superscripts.) Not only would these "words" have appeared in the basic word index (created from the title and abstract), but they would have been searched in a very cumbersome way using statements with proximity operators that indicate the sequence and the distance of the "words," such as "H w/1 2 w/1 SO w/1 4." This would have been embarrassingly unprofessional. The indexing of more than four million records had to be repeated after numeric characters were designated not to act as word separators.

Phrase (Term) Indexing

Phrase, or term, indexing is used when the entire contents of a field or subfield must appear as a unit in the index. It is used to retain the phrasal meaning of classification codes, book titles, journal names, subject headings, geographic names, and personal names. For example, Z681.3.067 as an LC classification code; Build Your Own Database as a title; Alzheimer's disease as a subject heading; O'Neill, Eugene as an author; and New England as a geographic name must all be retained as phrases. These are particularly useful when browsing the indexes because the users can see the entire term rather than its components such as "067," "Build," "Disease," "O," "Neill," "England," etc.[1] Actually, "England" would be explicitly misleading in a geographic name index when the entry refers to records with New England in the geographic location field.

Phrase indexing has limitations set by the software. Most typical is the limit on the length of the entry generated. If the limitation is too short, entries may be cut off before they become meaningful or distinctive units. For example, if the maximum length of the index entry (including the prefix) is twenty-seven characters, a corporate name such as Research Institute for the Advancement of Peace would have as its index entry "CS=Research Institute for t." Users certainly would wish the software would "drop the other shoe." In other cases the entry may lack a distinguishing identifier, for example, Series A.

One possible disadvantage of phrase indexing is that the searchers have to match the string exactly in their search query; that is, they must match at least up to a certain number of characters from the beginning to make the term distinctive enough. Given the inconsistent spelling, punctuation, abbreviations, and spacing in most of the databases that don't use authority control files, searching for exact matches for phrase-indexed data elements can be quite frustrating. This is especially true for corporate and journal names with inconsistently used abbreviations and punctuation.

Accented characters may pose special problems. Although accents may appear in the correct form in the record, they may not be preserved in creating the indexes. Even in Micro-CDS/ISIS, it is one thing to have the diacritical mark in the master records and it is another thing to have them in the index. In the indexes these marks disappear because the accented characters are replaced by their base character. This may also hinder hot-linking from a record to other records by the same author in the database. In some languages a word with and without the diacritics retains its meaning; the marks serve to indicate which syllable is stressed. In other languages words with and without an accent mark may have quite a different, often vulgar meaning. For example, in Hungarian *kar* is arm, and *kár* is damage.

Combined Word and Phrase Indexing

Browsing index entries—discussed in the next chapter—eases the task of finding relevant terms, but it cannot completely eliminate its drudgery. Phrase-indexed entries can be widely scattered in an index. To benefit from the advantages of the two main indexing methods, the software should allow the designer to create *both* a word and a phrase index for *each* data element chosen. This is useful when the user does not recall the title of a book or the name of the company. For example is it *Introduction to Computers in Libraries* or *Libraries and Computers—An Introduction?* Word indexing a title would generate an index entry for "Libraries," "Computers," and "Introduction" (assuming that *to, in, and,* and *an* are stop words). It could be retrieved by the combination of terms ("Introduction AND Libraries AND Computers") without recalling the exact title. Phrase indexing the title would generate one index entry that may be alphabetically distant from the title under which the user looks it up.

Similarly, word indexing journal titles can ease the pain of searching when it comes to titles whose elements may be abbreviated or whose punctuation may not be known. For example, there are quite a number of variations for such simple titles as *U.S. News and World Report: US News and World Report, US News & World Report, U.S. News and World Report,* and *U. S. News & World Report.* Longer titles, such as the *Journal of the American Society for Information Science* may appear in dozens of unpredictable variations. Word indexing the journal name field—along with truncation searching (discussed in the next chapter)—makes retrieving citations from specific journals much easier.

Prefixed Indexing

Beyond word and phrase indexing, another distinction is to add prefixes to the index entries. This is a very useful capability that indicates from what field the term was created. Internally, the software keeps track of this fact, but from the user's point of view, prefixed indexing will allow field-specific browsing. Prefixes collate entries that would be widely scattered from each other in an index without prefixes. The "CY=" index for country will put such entries as Holland, Netherlands, and The Netherlands relatively close to each other because only other country names come in between. These terms would be hundreds of screens away in an index that has no prefixes and that displays in a single index list all the index terms generated from different fields of the records.

Equally good are the indexes that, although they do not use visible prefixes, are invoked by clicking on a cell on the search template with a label such as "Countries." The index entries appearing in the drop-down menu are generated from the country data field. This is the approach taken in most of the microcomputer-based software.

Merged Indexing

The software should allow an index to be generated from several fields, acting as a generic index for a group of fields. In a serials database, for example, it is a wise idea to create a title index that culls its entries from various title fields. Users may not know and may not care if a title that they recall is a title proper, a former title, a successor title, a parallel title, a subtitle, an alternate title, or a spine title. They just want to search for it under title as a generic term. There can be another interface for staff members who may need to be able to search under the specific types of titles. EndNote Plus offers an elegant solution, allowing the designer to give an informative name for the index and to choose the fields from which a merged index will be generated. Equally intuitive is the way DB/TextWorks offers the list of fields to be used for generating the index terms. As shown in figure 6-2, the name of the index that can be chosen by the designer will be Authors. Entries for this index can be generated from the fields listed (Author, Secondary Author, Subsidiary Author, Tertiary Author). The designer decides which fields will be chosen to generate the merged index. The designer also chooses to use the Tertiary Author field for entering the name of the editor or the illustrator, for example.

Figure 6-2   Merged Index Creation in EndNote

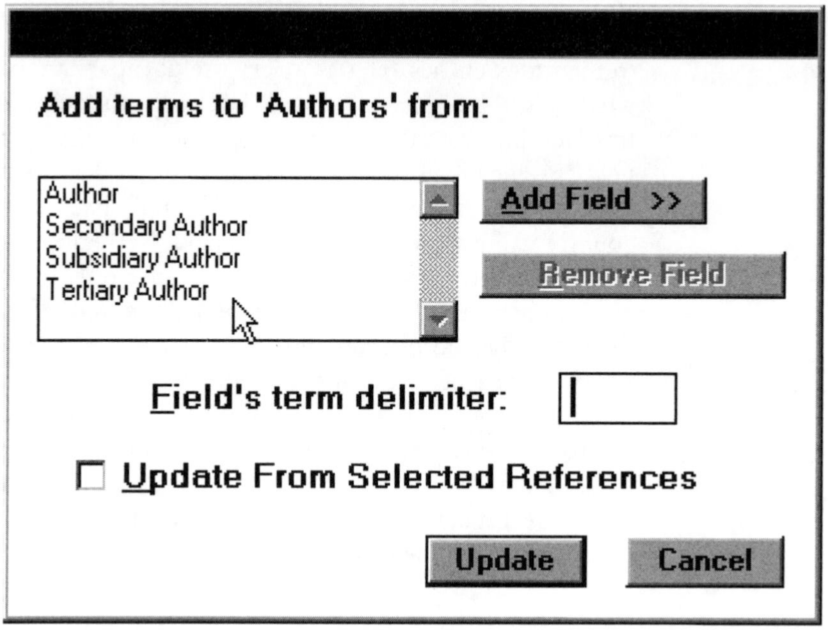

Absence/Presence Indexing

An unusual but very useful indexing feature of Micro-CDS/ISIS allows the designer to create an index entry based on the presence or absence of a field. In creating a directory database for a TV station for the archive documentaries, an important criterion was to be able to search for documentaries that won some award. The awards were listed in a repeatable field, but there was no need to search for specific awards. The field was not under authority control, and the entries were quite inconsistent in format. It would have been possible to add a single-character field to indicate if the documentary won an award, but with several thousand records it would have been quite time consuming. It was easier to generate an entry AW=YES if the field was present.

Similarly, in another project a legacy database was imported from another program that did not allow checking for the presence of mandatory fields during the original data entry. It was easy to generate prefixed indexes such as PY=NONE for those records that did not have the required

Figure 6-3   Search Based on the Absence/Presence of a Field in ProCite

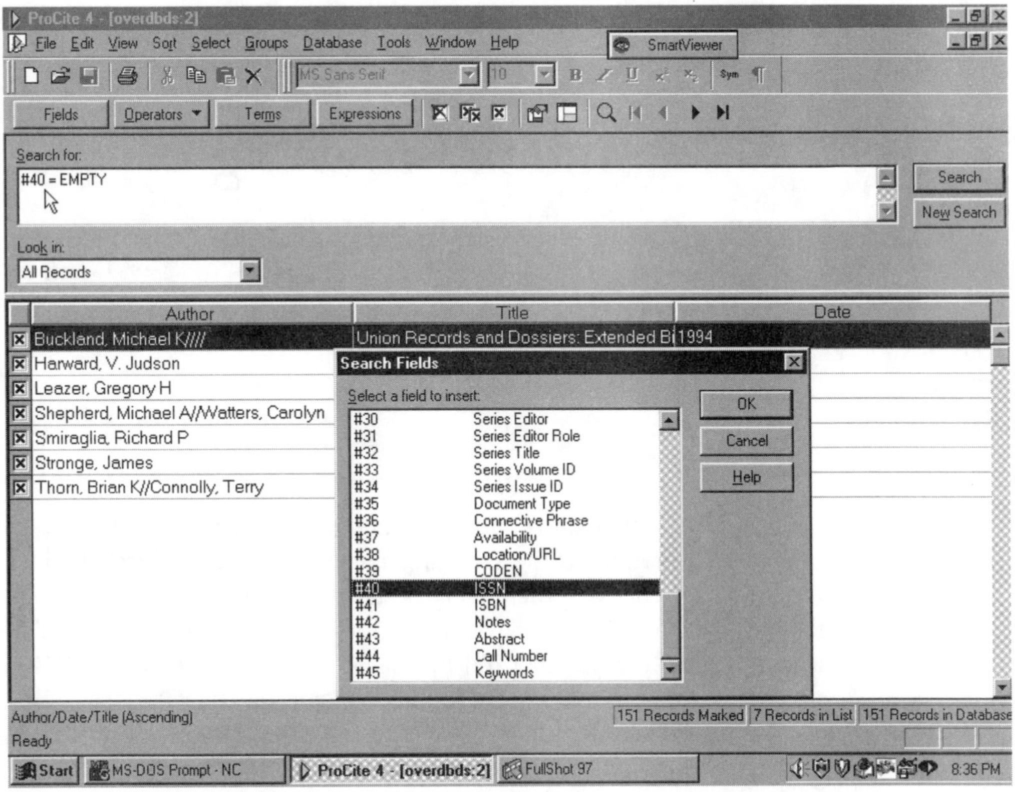

publication year and other mandatory fields. This helped the database maintenance staff to quickly select that subset of the records for corrections and enhancements in batches.

The need for finding records that have some information in a field must be common because ProCite has a feature that automatically generates an index that can be searched with the EMPTY and NOT EMPTY parameters. Figure 6-3 shows a ProCite search for records with the ISSN field empty.

Note   1. *Editor's note:* Throughout this text, search or indexing terms are enclosed in quotation marks to set them off as specific examples. Standard sentence punctuation is used within the quoted terms, such as commas within a series or ending sentence punctuation. These punctuation marks should not be considered part of the searching or indexing terms unless so specified.

7

Index Browsing

The flagship component of most textual database management software is the search module. If the software's data entry module does not offer good tools for checking the quality of data (as discussed in the previous chapters), the value of its search capabilities is significantly reduced. The same applies if the designer did not make use of the available sophisticated data-entry capabilities. Undoubtedly, some search features can compensate for inconsistent and inaccurate data entry both when picking search terms and when offering fuzzy searches or Soundex searches, where the search engine looks for similarly spelled or similarly sounding words. Still, the best prelude for a good search is browsing the indexes and picking index terms. Searching preceded by browsing is like selecting an item from a dessert trolley. Searching without browsing is like trying to describe the dessert that you would like to have.

The Reasons for Index Browsing

It is much easier to recognize a term such as "ophthalmology" or a name such as "Brzezinski, Zbigniew" than to enter it correctly. Typically, the users' search terms must match exactly the index terms letter by letter, space by space, and period by period. Even if the user knows how to spell a word or a name correctly, it does not ensure successful retrieval if the data entry operator misspelled the word or entered the name in correct but inconsistent formats. Misspellings in first names may seem to be a smaller problem than those in the surname, but in the case of a common surname, the first name and the middle initial can be the guiding factors in selecting the appropriate terms. Without the ability to browse indexes, many of the records would be missed.

It is quite telling that the following thirty variations of the *Journal of the American Oil Chemists' Society* were found in a single database. The variations may be minor for the human eye, and occasionally hard to spot, but for the computer software, all these are different entries:

J. AM OIL CHEM. SOC.

J. AM. OIL CHEM SOC.

J. AM. OIL CHEM. SOC.

J. AM. OIL CHEMISTS SOC.

J. AM. OIL. CHEM. SOC.

J. AMER OIL CHEMISTS SOC.

J. AMER OIL CHEMISTS' SOC.

J. AMER. OIL CHEMIST' SOC.

J. AMER. OIL CHEMIST'S SOC.

J. AMER. OIL CHEMISTRS' SOC.

J. AMER. OIL CHEMISTS SOC.

J. AMER. OIL CHEMISTS. SOC.

J. AMER. OIL CHEMISTS/ SOC.

J. AMER. OIL CHEMISTS' SOC

J. AMER. OIL CHEMISTS' SOC.

J. AMER. OIL CHEMISTS' SOC.,

J. AMER. OIL CHEMISTS'. SOC.

J. AMER. OIL CHEMISTS'S SOC.

J. AMER. OIL CHEMISTS'SOC

J. AMER. OIL CHEMISTS'SOC.

J. AMER. OIL. CHEMISTS' SOC

J. AMER. OIL. CHEMISTS' SOC.

J. AMER. OIL. CHEMISTS'SOC.

JAOCS - J. AM. OIL CHEM. SOC.

JAOCS, J. AM. OIL CHEM. SOC.

JOURNAL OF THE AMERICAN OIL CHEMISTS' SOC.

JOURNAL OF THE AMERICAN OIL CHEMISTS' SOCIETY

JOURNAL OF THE AMERICAN OIL CHEMISTS' SOCIETY.

JOURNAL OF THE AMERICAN OIL CHEMITS' SOCIETY

JOURNAL OF THE AMERICAN OIL CHEMITS'SOCIETY

Without browsing it would be impossible to gather all the variants. Some of them are scattered far away from the most-common formats. For example, JAOCS and the last five entries are likely to remain undiscovered even when browsing the indexes because the user may not think of looking at the acronym and fully spelled out versions. These are several screens apart from the rest, which more or less congregate. Similar patterns of inconsistency and inaccuracy exist with corporate and personal names as authors. Personal names are particularly important because they are very often used as access points. Index browsing may help to find items if there are typos at the end of the word rather than at the beginning and if there are minor inconsistencies in the punctuation between the first name and the middle initials.

Searching without browsing is not a good idea even if the terms are straightforward and simple and the database is clean. Without looking up a term, the user may not know, for example, that the preferred name of a journal title may include a qualifier such as the city of publication or that the author name may be qualified by his or her birth year or role as editor, compiler, etc.

Every field that is searchable should also be browsable. Many programs offer only predefined data elements for browsing. Others limit the choice to a few browsable indexes, but at least the designer can decide which ones to choose. The choice of browsable indexes is severely limited in many programs. Beyond the significant response time difference in searching indexed versus nonindexed fields, the lack of ability to look up terms for common search criteria such as publisher name, country, language of publication, or author affiliation significantly weakens the retrieval capabilities of users.

Index Types and Characteristics

As discussed in chapter 6, the two common ways to index data elements are word indexing and phrase indexing. From the searchers' perspectives the best indexing solution is to index a field both word by word and as a whole entry. Therefore, the journal *Information Technology and Libraries* generates entries for "technology," "libraries," and "Information Technology and Libraries." It should be possible to have the index entries generated with a prefix, that is, "JN=Information," "JN=Technology," "JN=Libraries," and "JN=Information Technology and Libraries." This option of choosing word and/or phrase indexing applies to substring indexing or subfield indexing.

The advantage of prefixed indexing (also known as field-specific indexing) is that it collocates the entries extracted from the same field and makes term selection much easier even if the word or term is misspelled. In a field-specific geographic name index it is easier to spot the misspelled versions of "Massachusetts" than in an overall keyword or basic index that lumps together words and terms generated from the title, abstract, descriptor, geographic location, and full-text fields.

Of course, if the field-specific index has thousands of unique entries, such as the author index, the scattering of terms may be too large even within the field-specific index to spot the wrong spelling: Lancester, F. W. There are too many intervening entries between Lancaster, F. W. and Lancester, F. W. to catch the wrong one via eyeballing the adjacent entries. The same is true for the common misspelling Jascó, Péter instead of Jacsó, Péter. The two entries may be dozens of screens apart.

Posting Information

Under any circumstance an essential feature of an index is its posting information. It tells the users in how many records the index entry occurs and provides an instant orientation if other terms should be selected to narrow or enhance the search without executing the search first. For example, if the term has a posting value of 14, the search may be initiated to retrieve those 14 records for reviewing. However, if the posting value is 3284, the search must be limited by including other terms, such as in the following statement:

(impeach? AND president?) NOT (Nixon OR Clinton)

The search statement in the preceding example will find records that include "impeach," "impeachment," "impeached," "impeaching" and "president," "presidents," and "presidential" but not those that include the name of either Nixon or Clinton.

Figures 7-1 through 7-4 show index entries from four different programs. Some indexes include posting information, such as shown in figure 7-1. Figures 7-2 through 7-4 do not include this information. A common index browsing deficiency of Reference Manager, EndNote, and Micro-CDS/ISIS (but not WinISIS) is the lack of posting information in the index. DB/TextWorks indexes include posting information. ProCite provides posting information only in the QuickSearch mode, a perfectly efficient mode of browsing and searching if it were not limited to the title, author, journal, and keyword fields.

It is a useful but not essential feature if the index includes posting information for the number of records and for the number of total occurrences. The number of records posting adds one posting for every record that has one or more occurrences of the word or term. The number of

Figure 7-1   Index Entries in DB/TextWorks

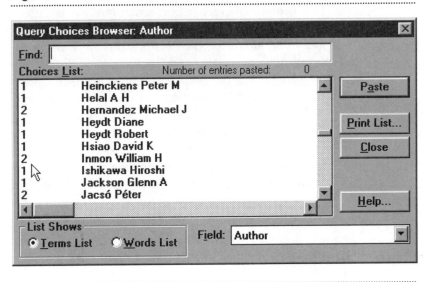

Figure 7-2   Index Entries in EndNote

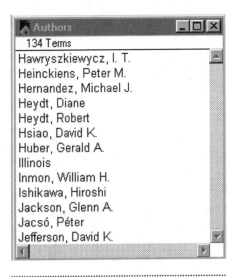

Figure 7-3   Index Entries in ProCite

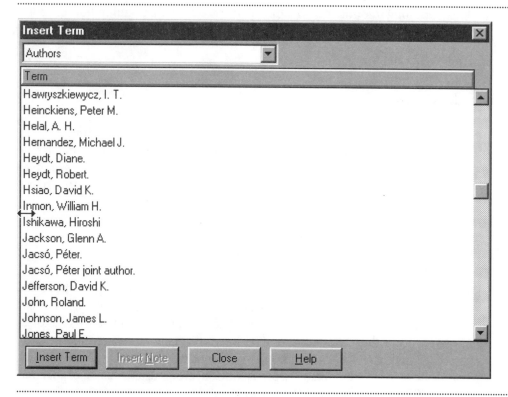

Figure 7-4   Index Entries in Reference Manager

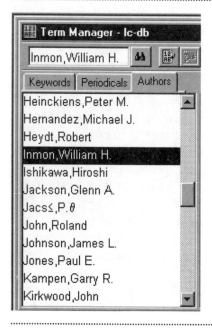

total occurrences posting counts every occurrence in calculating the posting information. The distinction is especially useful in full-text databases where a few records may contribute dozens of occurrences.

Term Selection

Very often the software allows users to select one term at a time. It is inconvenient because the user must pick one term and then initiate another browse operation for displaying the index and picking another term. This is particularly annoying when the user would like to choose adjacent terms. If the terms are adjacent due to singular and plural forms, choosing one term is not a problem because truncation can help. However, if the terms are adjacent because of internal spacing, punctuation differences, or errors that cannot be handled by truncation, then selecting multiple terms at once is essential.

Cross references can help users look up another term from the index. This assumes, of course, the use of controlled vocabulary. For example, the entry under "teenagers" could have a *see* reference to adolescents as the preferred term in a descriptor index. In a geographic index "Zaire" should include a *see also* reference to Congo, Democratic Republic of, or to Democratic Republic of Congo because the name changed in 1997 and both forms of entries are valid.

Thesauri are the ultimate tools in facilitating term selection. They show the family of related terms, including the broader (superordinated), narrower (subordinated), and the sidewise-related and preferred terms. None of the off-the-shelf software packages allow the creation of thesauri, though they are common with software running on mainframe computers and even on CD-ROMs published with proprietary programs that are not available for licensing.

CDS/ISIS offers an interesting compromise to using related terms. The database builder can create a list of terms and use a generic term to identify the list of related terms. The generic term then can be referred to with a special command that in turn would do a search for all the terms under the generic term. For example, the generic term "Hawaiian Islands" could include "Hawaii," "Maui," "Kauai," "Oahu," "Molokai," "Lanai," "Niihau," and "Kahoolawe." Instead of making the user enter all these terms and spell them correctly, the database publisher creates the list of these terms under the heading "@Hawaiian Islands." When the user selects this specially marked pseudo-index term, it will trigger a Boolean OR search for all the names listed under the group name.

This software feature came in handy in creating a variety of group terms for United Nations databases where users often needed to search by country names for sub-Saharan countries, SEATO countries, the Caribbean region, etc. This group-term feature could also be useful for the synonymous terms in a medical database such as postpartum, postnatal, puerperium, puerperal, after birth—to accommodate British, American, Latin, and lay-person terms.

As shown in figure 7-5, Reference Manager offers a somewhat similar solution. The developer of the database can assign 255 synonyms to a term. Using any of the synonyms will retrieve records that include any of the other synonyms. The feature applies only to the author, keyword, and journal name fields, and in the latter case the number of synonyms is limited to four. As opposed to the Micro-CDS/ISIS solution, the user does not need to enter any special command, so the synonyms feature could be used efficiently for grouping together predictable misspellings and inconsistent spellings of terms, as shown with the predictable name variations of one of the authors.

Figure 7-5   Reference Manager's Synonym Definitions

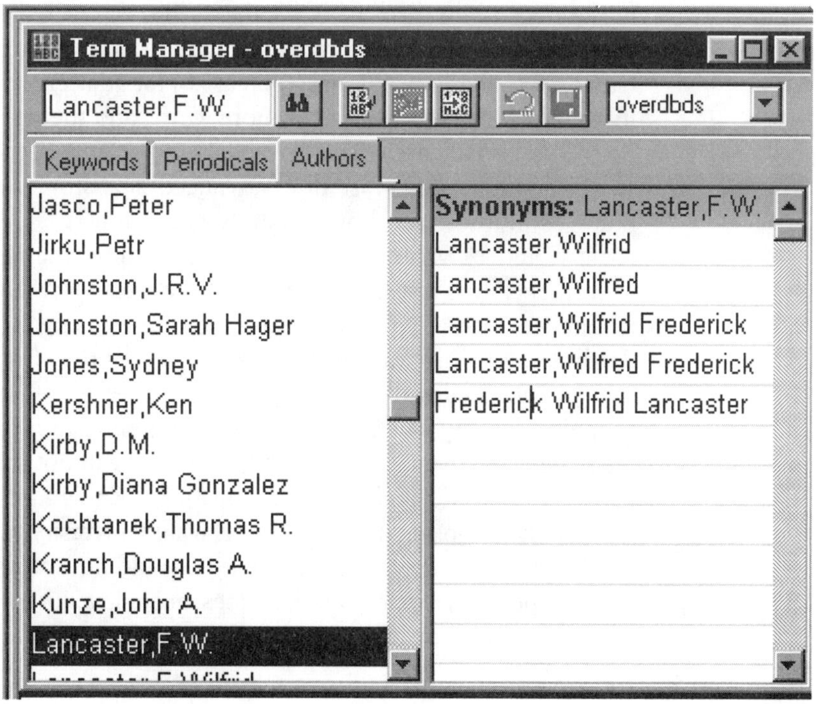

8

Searching

Searching preferably should be preceded by browsing to select one or more terms from the index before specifying the search statement. Whether entering search statements directly or after picking them from the index or thesaurus, users should be able to use essential operators to formulate the query.

The search operators that are absolutely essential, necessary, and useful depend on the type of databases and the experience of users. For example, abstracting and indexing databases don't mandate proximity (such as NEAR) and positional (such as ADJ for adjacent) operators to specify the distance between two or more words and their order, respectively. For full-text databases these are absolutely essential search operators.

In a public library setting, advanced operators are not needed as much as in a research library simply because it is less likely that casual users would be willing to learn the distinctions among the various advanced operators just to find a few books on a subject. On the other hand, researchers who are doing bibliometric studies using large citation-index databases certainly want to be able to use positional operators (such as ADJ) to make a clear distinction between University of Hawaii and Hawaii Pacific University when evaluating faculty publication patterns. The simple search statement "Hawaii AND University" will not achieve the desired result, as it would include both affiliations. Knowing that University of Hawaii often appears incorrectly as Hawaii University in databases, a positional operator between the two terms would not suffice either. Only the strictest positional operator that does not allow intervening words between the two terms may distinguish the two universities.

Boolean Operators

There are three basic Boolean operators that every software should offer: AND, OR, and NOT. These are used to search for records that have

term-1 OR term-2 OR term-3

term-1 AND term-2

term-1 NOT term-2

Searching with these operators is straightforward and simple—until the user has slightly more-complex requirements, such as finding every article published about literacy in Asia and Africa.

Assuming that the user can readily recognize that Asia and Africa should be translated into Asia OR Africa (as either is relevant), she could type in the search "Asia OR Africa AND literacy." Depending on the software this may yield a highly precise or grossly irrelevant result. The latter is the case when the software creates the sets by using precedence rules that specify that terms around the AND operator ("Africa AND literacy") are evaluated first followed by terms around the OR operator. The implication of this is that every record that has the terms "Africa" and "literacy" or has only the term "Asia" will be retrieved. If the search statement, however, is evaluated from left to right, it will retrieve records that have either "Asia" or "Africa" and the word "literacy." It will also pick up records that have all three words, such as the one with the title "Literacy Rates in Asia, Africa and Oceania Improve."

The software should offer the option to use parentheses to override the precedence, that is, to specify "(Asia OR Africa) AND literacy." Another question is whether the user is aware of the precedence rules or recognizes the reason for irrelevant records.

Using the NOT operator may further complicate the search. The NOT operator is usually in the last part of the search statement, but it may be evaluated prior to the other two operators. For example, the search statement "Asia OR Africa AND literacy NOT South Africa" may pick up all the records about Asia or Africa except those that discuss literacy in South Africa. It may yield more irrelevant records than the previous statement when in reality the user wanted to focus the search, as in ((Asia OR Africa) AND literacy) NOT South Africa.

Though these simple Boolean operators may do harm occasionally, they are still essential. Natural-language-based search engines (discussed later in this chapter) always emphasize as their advantage that users do not need to know Boolean operators. It is not that the Boolean operators are hard to understand but that their various interpretations are complex.

A help file may alleviate the problem through good examples, but the software should offer these operators.

A fourth operator, the exclusive OR (also known as XOR), is rarely needed in practice. The statement "(Asia XOR Africa) AND literacy" would find records in which either Asia or Africa occurs along with literacy but would exclude those records that have both Asia and Africa, such as the one shown previously: "Literacy Rates in Asia, Africa and Oceania Improve."

EndNote, DB/TextWorks, and the Windows version of Micro-CDS/ISIS (WinISIS) offer a template for entering Boolean statements. In EndNote clicking on a radio button specifies the relationship between the search items. (See figure 8-1.) In DB/TextWorks the Boolean buttons are labeled. (See figure 8-2.) Clicking on a button will rotate the label among AND, OR, and NOT. Reference Manager uses a similar approach, but the cell for the Boolean operators is not really intuitive because the user is not given a hint about what to enter in the Connector cell. The leftmost cell with the column label Connector must be clicked on to bring up the Boolean options. (See figure 8-3.) EndNote's and WinISIS' approaches seem to be the most intuitive. (See figure 8-4.) ProCite has

Figure 8-1   Boolean Query in EndNote

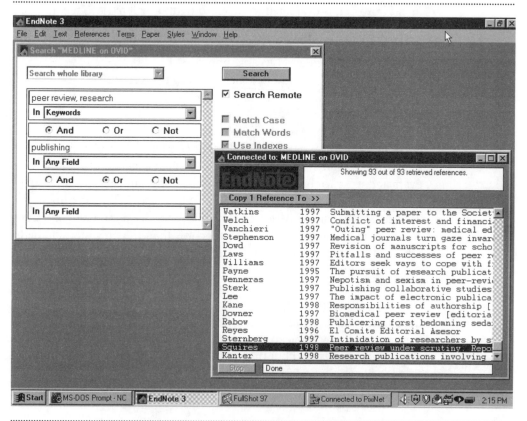

Figure 8-2   Boolean Query in DB/TextWorks

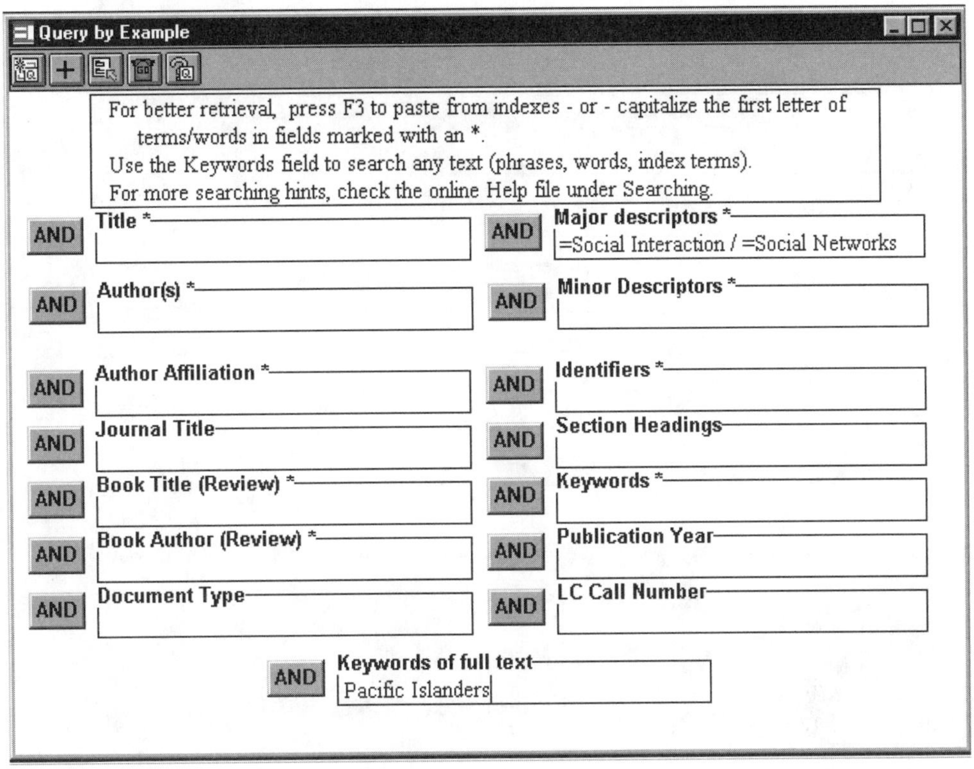

Figure 8-3   Boolean Query in Reference Manager

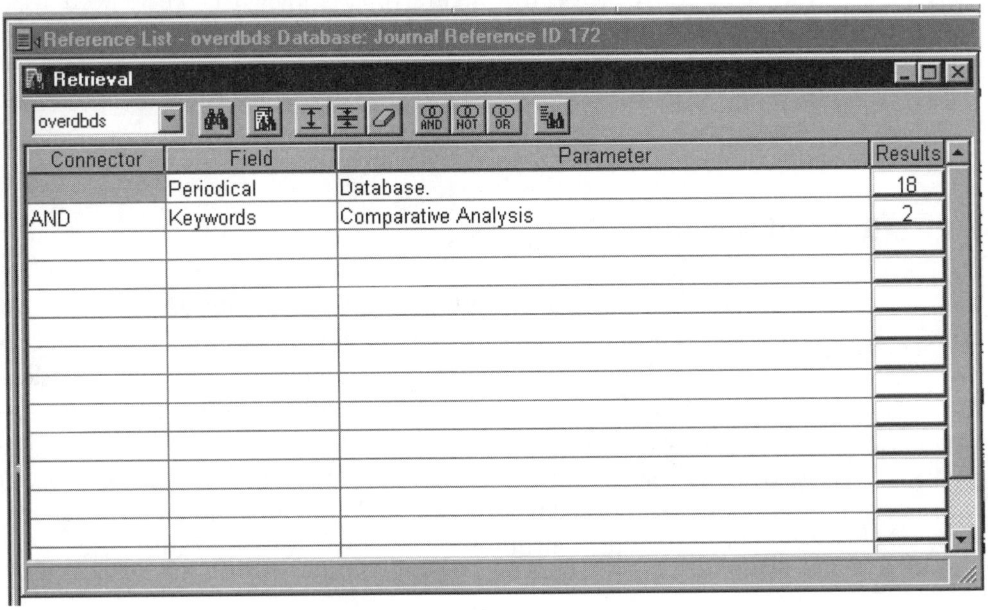

Figure 8-4   Boolean Query in WinISIS

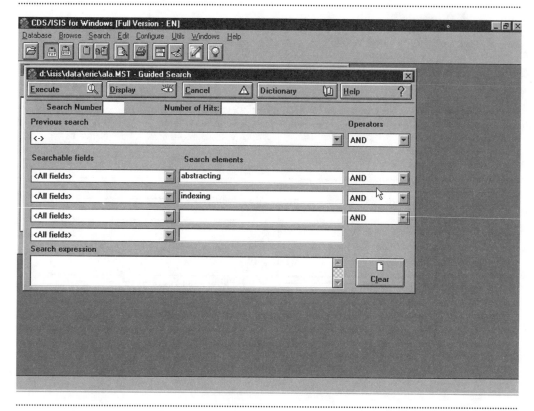

too many operators to use radio buttons or labeled buttons, so it offers a nice pull-down menu. (See figure 8-5.) Somewhat experienced users may directly type in the request, such as Author = Lancaster AND keyword = abstracting.

Truncation and Masking

Truncation is a convenient feature to find terms with different endings. Using the asterisk character as a truncation symbol, "librar*" would retrieve "library," "librarian," "librarians," "librarianship," and "libraries." Most programs offer this unlimited truncation. Fewer programs make distinctions between exact and unlimited truncation, though it may be important, especially with short stems. Using the question mark for exact truncation, "art?" would retrieve "art" and "arts" but not "artifact," "artery," "arthritic," "arthritis," "arthrosis," "artichoke," "article," "artist," etc.

Figure 8-5   Pull-Down Menu for Boolean Query in ProCite

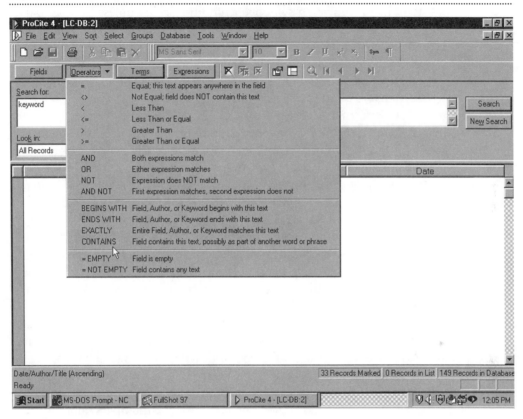

Exact truncation may be interpreted by the software literally that one character must follow the stem of the word, so "art" itself would not be retrieved with the search for "art?". It is more common, however, that exact truncation means truncating one character or none. A further variation is using several exact truncation characters to specify up to how many characters can follow the stem. For example, "art????" would retrieve "art," "artery," "artful," "article," "artist," "artists," and "arts" but not "artistic," "artifice," or other words that follow the stem with more than four characters.

Truncation can be to the right or left, though most programs allow only right truncation. Depending on the content of the database, left truncation may be useful but not essential. For examples, in an art database it is handy to be able to specify "French AND paint* AND *ism" to find various movements in French painting from pointillism to impressionism to dadaism. In a medical database left truncation may be needed to search for local anesthetics such as procaine, butacaine, benzocaine, and other "caine" anesthetics. The ability to search for "*caine" in ProCite is undoubtedly very useful.

EndNote searches for a term as a character string (adding left and right hand truncation symbols behind the scene) unless the user clicks on the Exact Word option. This automatic bidirectional truncation can retrieve very irrelevant items such as "design," "designer," or "designing" for "sign" as a search term. It would be better not to assume truncation on both sides but to offer either a "contain" box (as ProCite does), if indeed that is wanted, or truncation symbols.

In Reference Manager the lack of "field democracy" has a confusing effect on truncation searching. Truncation can be used in the special fields (author, journal name, and keyword), but it must not be used in the other fields. To add to the confusion, whole words must be searched by adding a space after the word; for example, "art " must be entered when searching for the word *art* in the title. However, this would not retrieve those occurrences of the word *art* when it is followed by a comma, a period, a question mark, or any other punctuation mark. Such instances of following punctuation must be specified separately in the query for a complete retrieval unless the user chooses to create automatically an entry for the keyword index from the title field. Truncation may be used in the keyword index.

Masking is often called internal truncation, but it is not an appropriate term. Something can be truncated on one or both ends but not within. Masking offers the users the choice of ignoring one or more characters within a word. This is very useful for some British and American spelling differences. For example, "organi?ation" would retrieve both "organisation" and "organization." Some programs require multiple symbols if multiple characters need to be masked. In either case, there are subvariations in which the masking may be exact or up to the specified number of characters including none. For many differences in British and American spelling the "up to" method is better. This way "arch?eolog*" would retrieve "archeological," "archeologist," "archeologists," and "archeology" as well as "archaeological," "archaeologist," "archaelogists," and "archaeology."

Case Sensitivity

Most programs are not case sensitive in searching. "ALA" or "ala" would retrieve the same number of records. This is a good search assumption, especially with the proliferation of lowercasing everything on the Web, including personal names and signatures. Case insensitivity makes most searchers—and would have made e. e. cummings—happy except when searching for terms that have a different meaning in upper-, lower-, and mixed-case formats. One may search for "National Organization of

Women" in its spelled-out format, but it is certainly simpler just to type in "NOW" and click on the case sensitivity button in EndNote. The same applies to searching for articles about the acronyms AIDS or SALT. This would not work, however, for finding articles about the NeXT computer of Steve Jobs. Specifying case sensitivity on those occasions when it makes a difference is a wise solution.

Field Qualification

Searches can be made much more precise if one or more of the search terms are restricted to certain fields of the record. This is relevant only for those programs that create combined indexes, often known as basic indexes or keyword indexes, from several data elements. Lumping terms from several fields into one index can be advantageous as long as there is a possibility to qualify the search when needed.

For example, in a serials directory it is a good idea to create an index that includes the titles and/or the title words from various kinds of title fields such as title proper, subtitle, key title, parallel title, variant title, cover title, spine title, former title, successor title, etc. The patron may not remember whether a title was the cover title or the key title, and he or she does not really care as long as the journal is easily found. If the journal title changed and the record of the new title is brought up, the patron may learn about the current title.

However, for technical services people it may be necessary to limit a search to the title proper field. It is useful to qualify the search by limiting the search to the title proper field, such as "CD-ROM Professional/TP" or "TP=CD-ROM Professional" to avoid retrieving the records of Laserdisk Professional and EMedia Professional (its former and successor titles, respectively).

Field qualification is necessary to avoid retrieving irrelevant hits in a full-text database that tangentially mentions a concept. The ability to restrict the search to the title field or the descriptor field can reduce the number of records retrieved and increase the relevance of the hits. If the search can be restricted to several fields at a time, for example, to either the title or the descriptor field, searches are more efficient. A variation of this approach is to restrict the search to the major descriptor field to further focus the search. If field qualification is possible, it is a design issue. Restricting to major descriptors assumes that the items are indexed at two levels by assigning descriptors as being major or minor, and the database stores them in two different fields or distinguishes them with a special character. The asterisked descriptors in the following records are the major descriptors; that is, the concepts described by these descriptors are emphasized in the document. The minor descriptors (without asterisks) are not the focal points of the article. A minor descriptor for one document can be a major descriptor for another and vice versa.

TI: The Relationship of Bibliographic Database Design to the Structure of Information: A Case Study in Education.

DE: *Bibliographic Databases; *Bibliographic Records; *Database Design; Educational Research; Foreign Countries

The alternative approach is to put the major (DJ) and minor (DM) descriptors in different fields:

TI: The Relationship of Bibliographic Database Design to the Structure of Information: A Case Study in Education.

DJ: Bibliographic Databases; Bibliographic Records; Database Design

DM: Educational Research; Foreign Countries

Field qualification is possible with both prefixes and suffixes. For the former example about CD-ROM Professional, it is possible that a program favors the prefixed searching, such as "TP=CD-ROM Professional" or multiple-prefixed searching for the latter example: "DJ, DM=database*" to find records in which the word "database" or "databases" appears either as major (DJ) or minor (DM) descriptors. A shortcut could be created for searching both the major and minor descriptors by creating a combined index from both fields with the DE= prefix or suffix, making these two fields searchable as in "DE=database*" or "database*/de."

The preceding two examples illustrate field-specific searching in command mode. These days the most common approach to offering field qualification is through a template and pull-down menu combination. Instead of potentially cryptic prefixes and suffixes, the complete field name may be displayed on a pull-down menu, and the selection of the field values will be limited to the selected index.

ProCite and especially Reference Manager are parsimonious with browsable indexes. However, both programs allow searching all the fields that make up the record. (See figures 8-6 and 8-7.) Many of the fields are not indexed; therefore, searching will be slower than if they were indexed. However, the search terms may be limited to a particular field. Moreover, both programs automatically generate compound indexes from the different author fields: Author, Analytic; Author, Monographic; Author, Subsidiary and Series Editor in ProCite; and Authors, Primary; Authors, Secondary; and Authors, Series in Reference Manager. These indexes can be also be searched on their own, for example, to find all the books of F. W. Lancaster for which he is the primary author. Such combined indexes also are automatically created for the various title and date fields by these two programs.

Figure 8-6   Field-Specific Searching in ProCite

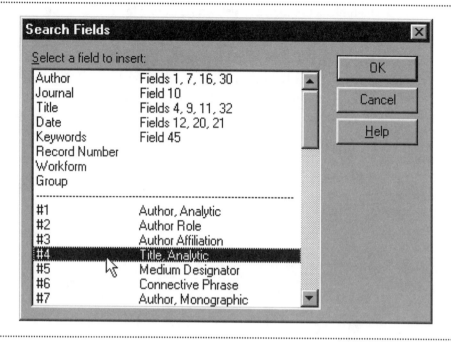

Figure 8-7   Field-Specific Searching in Reference Manager

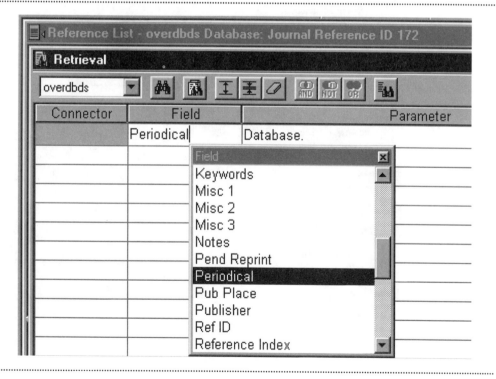

EndNote offers a more flexible approach, letting the user define which fields to index and determine from which fields a combined index will be created. This makes it possible, for example, to create a minor descriptor index, a major descriptor index, and a combination of both. The freedom to choose one's indexes makes it possible, for example, to create an index (and a browsable index at that) for the publisher field in EndNote, something that is not possible in ProCite and Reference Manager. (See figure 8-8.) The publisher field is searchable in both those programs but not through an index; therefore, searches are much slower than those in EndNote.

Figure 8-8   Field-Specific Searching in EndNote

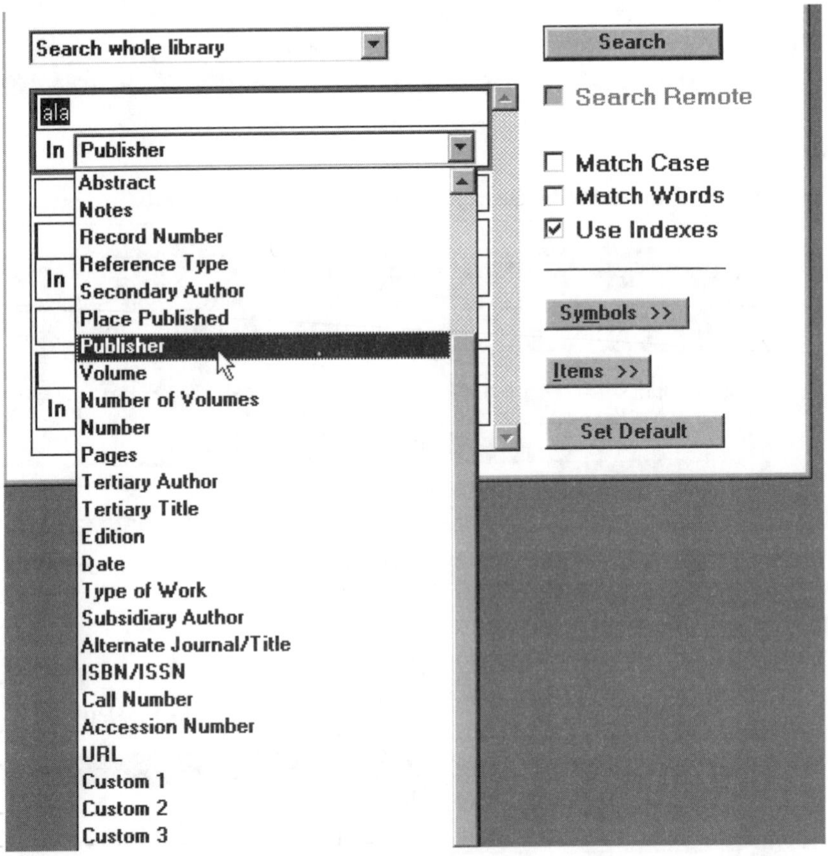

DB/TextWorks and Micro-CDS/ISIS offer additional flexibility. The designer can create more than one type of index for any of the fields (for example, a word index and phrase index with and without prefixes) and may use one or several fields to generate the entries. Users may choose any of these indexes; they are not limited only to those combined indexes made available automatically by the software. (In contrast, ProCite and Reference Manager limit searches to combined indexes.) Furthermore, DB/TextWorks and Micro-CDS/ISIS allow users to specify in a single search statement several field qualifiers, much like improvised field qualification. In one application this flexibility was used to create a combined Credit field from the actor, director, and producer fields in addition to their individual indexes. In turn, the user could search in the Credit field for the person in any of the three capacities, in the Actor index alone, or in the Actor and Screenwriter indexes as an improvised combined index. In the example in figure 8-9 the word "software" must appear in the title and the author's name must be Jacsó Péter (as an exact phrase without a comma as indicated by the = sign). In the example in figure 8-10 the author must include the name with the prefix exactly, with a comma (as indicated by the double quotes), and the word "databases" must appear in one of the indexed fields (indicated by the <All fields> label). This search statement entered in the template is then translated by the program into a search command that appears in the lower window as a confirmation, so users are likely to learn the syntax of the command mode search sooner or later.

Figure 8-9   Field-Specific Searching in DB/TextWorks

Figure 8-10   Field-Specific Searching in WinISIS

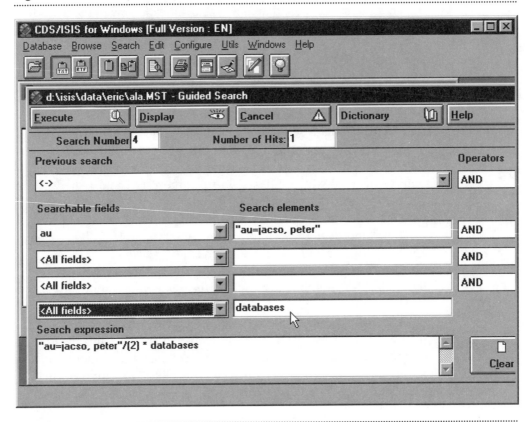

Proximity and Positional Operators

The availability of proximity and positional operator features is essential mostly in full-text databases, and is useful for databases that have long abstracts or in databases on which very precise searches must be done for bibliometric studies. These searches require, for example, the capability to define the order and sequence of two or more search terms to tell apart "University of Oregon" and "Oregon State University" in the author affiliation field. (If the field is phrase indexed and browsable and abbreviations and punctuation are consistently used in the field, there is no need for proximity and positional operators. The appropriate terms may be picked from the browsable index.)

Proximity operators allow users to specify how far two or more of the terms should be from each other to qualify for retrieval. The proximity or adjacency operators typically specify the distance in terms of words, that is, up to one word apart, two words apart, etc. This is a reasonable measure, but there are other alternatives. Additional proximity operators include distance in terms of characters or whether words appear within the same sentence, the same paragraph, or the same field. The more variety there is, the more flexibly the search can be adjusted for precision and recall.

Proximity operators can preserve bound (or compound) terms to be retrieved as a concept even if only word indexing is possible. It is easy to search for articles about New Mexico if an adjacency operator is available such as "New ADJ Mexico" or "New (N) Mexico" that specifies that no intervening words can be between the two words. (The meaning of these operators varies among programs; they may imply an even more strict requirement to be discussed later in this section.) Such proximity requirements ensure retrieval of something about New Mexico rather than something new in Mexico that looser proximity operators, such as sentence proximity or paragraph proximity, cannot achieve.

In some cases specifying proximity is not enough. The position of the words to each other should be also specified to achieve high precision. For example, "library school" and "school library" can be distinguished only if positional operators are also offered by the software. Positional operators provide refinement in the New Mexico example where only the adjacency of the two terms was required but not their position relevant to each other. Using "New (w) Mexico" can eliminate those false hits where one sentence ends and the other begins like this: ". . . violent crime increased in Mexico. New legislation is expected."

In some programs the absolute proximity and positional operation can be achieved by putting the compound term between quotes, such as "database design." Obviously, this is not ideal because this exact search would not find the plural form (databases) and the inflected versions (designer, designing, etc.). Nor is this exact adjacency appropriate when variations that are to be searched include terms such as "drug abuse"; "drug and alcohol abuse"; and "drug, alcohol, and tobacco abuse." For searches such as these, slightly looser proximity is required, and the order of the terms should also be loosened to retrieve "abuse of drugs." For example, the search statement "drug? (3N) abuse?" could be appropriate as it allows for the variants "drug," "drugs," "abused," "abuser," and "abusers" (but not abusing) and allows the terms to appear in either order with up to three intervening words.

Proximity and positional operators cannot completely eliminate false hits. For example, a search for articles about library school programs should not specify the exact word order, such as "library (W) school? (W) program?," because it would not retrieve records that mention the program of a library school. The search "library (W) school (2N) program?" loosens the search by allowing the word "program" to appear before or after the term "library school." However, such a search statement still would not retrieve the record that mentions the program of School of Library and Information Studies. This would require a looser statement of the relation between "library" and "school" by allowing the two words to be in any order although next to each other with one intervening word (of). However, such a statement would also retrieve many irrelevant records about school library programs. This may seem to be an extreme example, but in full-text databases in which the software allows truncation, searchers may easily run into such dilemmas. The answer boils down to the issue of recall versus precision, and the software should support the user's effort to optimize either strategy. Few microcomputer programs offer positional and proximity operators. In the sample group only DB/TextWorks has both proximity and positional operators, and Micro-CDS/ISIS has proximity options, rather obscure ones at that.

The (G) operator between two search terms specifies that the first term must appear in the same field as the second term, for example, "headache (G) diet therapy."

The (F) operator specifies that the first and second term must appear in the same occurrence of the field. This can be a very useful operator for the MEDLINE database where the MeSH term and its subdivision may need to be searched together for increased relevance. For example, "headache (F) diet therapy" will retrieve only those records in which diet therapy is the subheading for headache. Records in which "headache" occurs with "drug therapy," and those in which "diet therapy" is the subheading for the subject heading "weight loss" would not be retrieved because the search terms are not in the same occurrence of the MeSH field.

In the WinISIS program, the number of periods (.) as operators specify up to how many words may appear between two search terms. Alternatively, the number of dollar signs ($) specify how many words must be exactly between two search terms. This is as strict as it gets, and it is not intuitive in the otherwise very user-friendly WinISIS system.

These positional and proximity operators are likely to be featured in the next versions of most of the database management programs. The availability of free or inexpensive full-text documents on the Web and the plummeting hard-drive costs will motivate users to download and store full-text documents and search them efficiently.

Simplicity and intuitivity may be the most important factors for many users in doing efficient proximity and positional searches. ProCite has a remarkably effective browse-and-search mode, called QuickSearch, that is perfect when there is no need for the power-search options. It lets the user browse one of a few indexes and pick a term. In turn, on the same screen one or more records in short format appear in a pane. Clicking on one of the short-entry records will display the full record. (See figure 8-11.) All this happens on the same screen instantly, and it could not be more intuitive. Some users are, however, satisfied only with natural-language software.

Figure 8-11 QuickSearch in ProCite

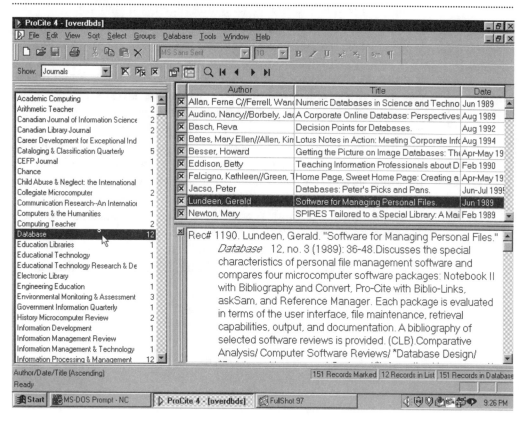

Natural-Language Searching and Relevance Ranking

Natural-language searching has been heralded as the panacea for the problems of understanding and learning the syntax and semantics of Boolean operators, truncation, masking, field qualification, and proximity and positional operators. Search engines that accept natural-language queries use many of these techniques behind the scenes. Typically, such search engines retrieve a large number of records that include one or more terms presented in the query. In essence the first step is a Boolean OR operation enhanced with one type of truncation and—rarely—a masking operation. This subset of the database is then ranked by relevance as perceived by the search engine.

The ranking algorithms are not published in detail but can be guessed after some well-targeted test searches. Many programs give the highest rank to those records that include the most terms from the query. Others refine this strategy by assigning different weights to terms depending on how often they occur in the entire database. Those records that have a higher score based on the frequency of occurrence and the weight of the terms get a higher rank. Others give higher rank to terms that occur in the title or descriptor fields or in the lead paragraph (in the case of full-text databases). Yet others rank the records based on the proximity of two or more of the search terms. A few search engines combine several of these ranking criteria.

There have been improvements in the algorithms of search software that accept natural-language queries, but they certainly should not be presented as an exclusive solution. The ideal software should offer both command-language and natural-language options. None of the sample programs discussed in this book have natural-language capabilities. Those programs that have such capabilities have been very well received, such as PLS (Personal Library Software). However, PLS does not have nearly as sophisticated data entry and output capabilities as the sample programs.

9

Sorting

Sorting of results is an often-neglected area of textual database management software. This is odd because a good sort module could compensate for the search deficiency of a program. If the result of a search can be easily sorted by, say, journal name, the retrieval of the original documents from the shelf is far more efficient than a run-of-the-mill sorting based on decreasing data-entry date. Data-entry date sorting is often claimed to be decreasing publication year sorting simply because it is likely that the most recently added records are for the most recently published materials. However, this is not always the case when, for example, foreign materials are also included or when correction records or records for formerly missed conference papers are added to a database much later than the original publication year. Conference proceedings are notorious for being published several months or even years after the presentation of papers. It might happen that the first results of a data-entry date search include two-year-old conference papers that were just added to the database.

Result lists that are presented in a spreadsheet format are very efficient. All three bibliography management programs display the result list in this format. ProCite and Reference Manager offer a convenient way of sorting the results list by simply clicking on the header of the column. (See figure 9-1.) If the chosen sort criterion is not distinct, that is, if the author appears more than once, then these programs use their default secondary and tertiary criteria. The user has control only over the primary sort criterion.

EndNote has a pop-up window that allows the user to specify five levels of sort criteria. Each of them can be in ascending or descending order. (See figure 9-2.)

Figure 9-1 Sorted Result List in ProCite

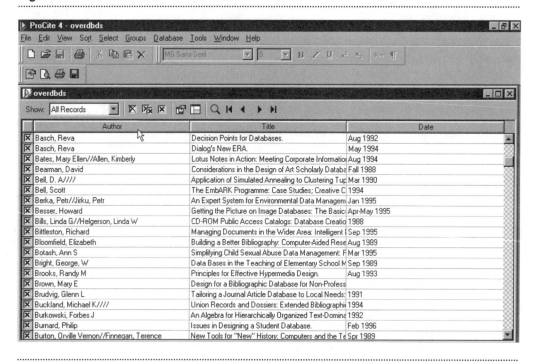

Figure 9-2 Sorted Result List in EndNote

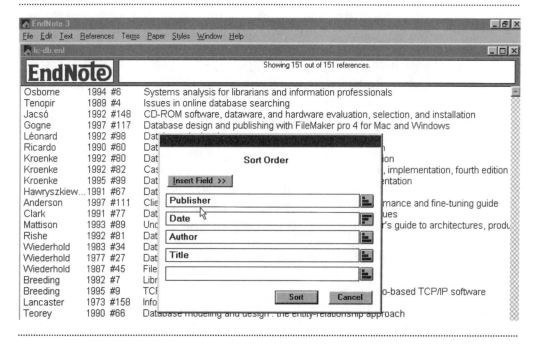

DB/TextWorks does not have a spreadsheet-like results list, but the database designer may create one and apply the same sort features as for the full report. WinISIS does not offer sorting at the results list level or for screen display at all. Instead, it provides sort options only for printed output.

More-sophisticated features in most of the software are used to sort a bibliography. Many are intuitive and menu driven, except for WinISIS. Although that program has the most-sophisticated sort options of the sample software, it is a very complex process even in the Windows environment. The following sections discuss the most important criteria for evaluating the sort capabilities.

Choice and Number of Sort Keys

The choice of the sort keys is often limited to title, author, and publication year. The software should let the designer or the end user choose the data elements by which the results are to be sorted. Instead of—or in addition to—sorting by these three data elements, users may want to list the records by journal name, standard industry classification code, subject headings, section codes, LC classification codes, etc.

Typically, not only the choice of fields but also the number of sort keys that can be defined are limited. This means that although most of the fields can be designated as sort keys, no more than two or three of these can be chosen. Most software packages allow a primary and a secondary level of sort key, for example, sorting first by journal name and then by publication year. Without the stretch of imagination it is quite feasible that someone would like to sort the results also by the name of the author as a third-level criterion. ProCite offers up to six sort levels (depending on the document types sorted); EndNote offers five levels; Reference Manager offers a relatively meager three levels. All of these bibliography formatting programs, however, have built-in sort orders that are defined by the styles used for creating the bibliography, such as the ANSI (American National Standard Institute), APA (American Psychological Association), or the Chicago Manual of Style. (See figures 9-3 through 9-5.) In DB/TextWorks and WinISIS, the designer may create as complex sort specifications as may be required, including five levels of sort and a number of other options discussed in the following sections.

Usually, the software packages stop at offering a few fields of sorting, but the programs in the sample (especially ProCite, DB/TextWorks, and—for printed output only—WinISIS) offer extraordinary sort capabilities that are very useful when the result of database searches should be presented in the form of a professional bibliography or catalog.

Figure 9-3   Sort Template in ProCite

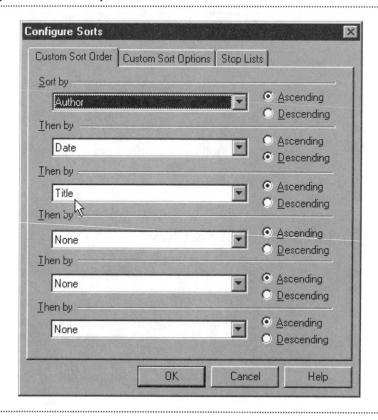

Figure 9-4   Sort Template in EndNote

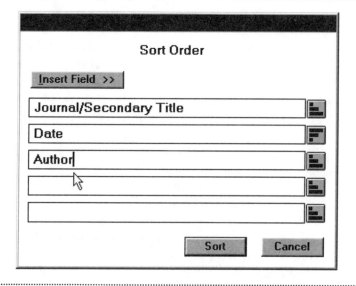

Figure 9-5   Sort Template in Reference Manager

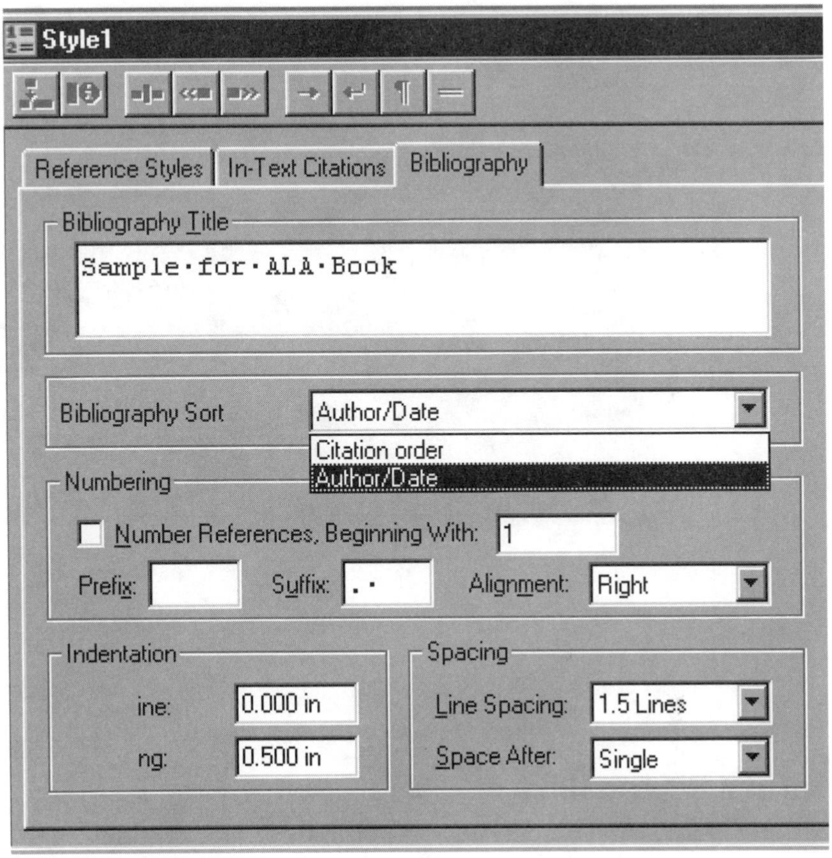

Alternate Sort Fields

When the designated sort field is absent from the record, the program should offer the choice of an alternate or "understudy" field that takes its place. This is a very common occurrence, for example, when records are to be sorted by author; if author data is not available, the record should be sorted by title. This is the way author/title catalogs have been manually created. DB/TextWorks offers an intuitive menu to specify the alternate sort field. ProCite offers a more modest option to let the user decide if records for which the sort field is absent should be sorted prior to or after the rest of the records. This helps to override the built-in algorithm of the software, but is no substitute for the alternate field options of DB/TextWorks and WinISIS. (See figure 9-6.)

Figure 9-6   Specifying an Alternate Sort Field in DB/TextWorks

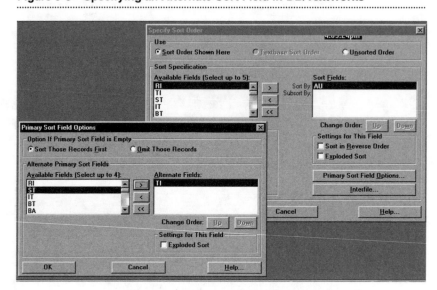

Sorting Repeated Sort Fields

If the field used as a sort criterion is a repeatable field, the user should be able to choose between two alternatives. One is to sort the record under the first occurrence of the sort field, such as the primary author. The other alternative is to have full records under each author. A variation of the first alternative is to have a full entry under the first author and a short entry (to be defined by the designer or user), such as title and pub-lication year, under the rest of the authors or just the authors' names with a *see* reference to the primary author. WinISIS offers all these possi-bilities. DB/TextWorks offers either sorting by all the occurrences of a field (choosing the Explode box on the sort menu) or only by the first occurrence. (See figure 9-7.)

ProCite allows sorting by all the authors or by the first author only, but it limits this sort option to the author field. Sorting by repeated fields is also essential for bibliographies arranged by subject headings, classifica-tion codes, or publishers. As an extra, ProCite also allows the choice to sort only by the last name or the full name of the authors. (See figure 9-8.)

Figure 9-7   DB/TextWorks Explode Sort Feature of Author Field

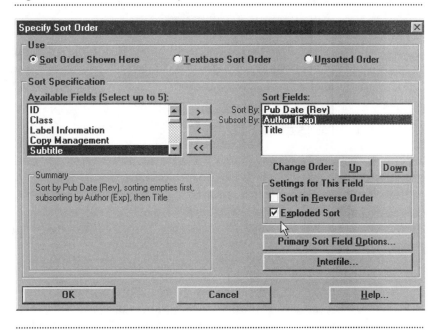

Figure 9-8   Sorting by All Authors in ProCite

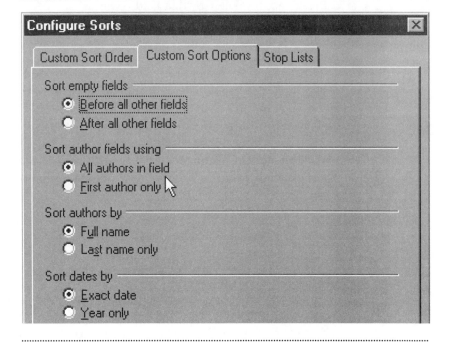

Number Sorting

Numbers are often treated as normal character strings in bibliographic information management software. This implies that numbers are compared from left to right, one character at a time. The result is the following inappropriate sort order:

1

157

2

201

3

Using leading zeros can alleviate the problem, but it may make the printed record look odd. For example, in creating a table of contents record, the start page of the articles would have to be filled with leading zeros (such as 002, 018, etc., for a book that has no more than 999 pages) to sort the record with a starting page number of 157 after the records with starting page numbers of 2 and 18. ProCite, for example, has only one truly numeric field, the call number field, that could appropriately sort the numeric values. If that field is used for the call number, then any other numeric field must be entered with leading zeros to sort the result appropriately by that field.

DB/TextWorks offers the most flexible handling of numbers for sorting and for numerical computations. If a field is defined as numeric (and any field can be defined as such), it can be sorted by numeric value even if the number is preceded or followed by text. For example, "ordered 5 copies" and "5 copies ordered" will be appropriately sorted by the numeric value or used in a calculation. The number field can also handle negative numbers, a rarity in textual information management software.

DB/TextWorks also excels in handling the special numeric format of classification codes that mix numbers and alphabetic and special characters. This feature makes it the perfect candidate when records must be sorted by LC, Dewey, or UDC codes.

Date Sorting

Dates play a special role in sorting because they can be entered in many different ways and because they are often needed as primary and secondary search criteria. Dates represent a special category of number fields. Mainstream database management software can handle date fields quite flexibly, but textual information management systems often fail to offer a solution to sort, for example, "December, 1998" after "November, 1998" when they appear in this spelled-out format. Of course, this problem can be avoided if all the dates are consistently entered in structured numeric date format, such as YYYY/MM/DD—assuming that leading zeros are used, for example, 2000/01/01 for January 1, 2000. The year-2000 problems made many developers regret the decision to use only two digits for the year, and among the many potential problems caused by this convention, sorting is only a minor one. ProCite can sort the date fields as exact date (comparing as much date information as is entered in the field) or by year only. DB/TextWorks offers utmost flexibility in handling dates, even allowing some nondate text following the date such as "31 December, 1999 [claimed for the second time]" and still consider it a date field.

Sorting Special Characters

The appearance of special characters such as quotes, apostrophes, and parentheses in the beginning of a title typically upsets the correct sort order in most of the software. In some databases these special characters may be removed, but sometimes they have special meaning, such as indicating information added to rather than taken from the source. For example, "[Democratic Republic of] Congo" would be incorrectly filed ahead of "AAA Guide to Hawaii" because the internal code values that are used to represent these symbols are lower than those for the alpha characters. Similarly, a title like "'Understudy' Fields for Correct Sorting of Records" would be the first item in the bibliography sorted by title. Few programs handle these special characters appropriately. ProCite removes any characters other than letters and numbers for sorting purposes, but it retains them for displaying and printing. This is a good solution. Micro-CDS/ISIS offers the use of a pair of special symbols that should surround the character string to be ignored in sorting, whether it is a single special character or an entire word. This is discussed at the end of this section.

Accented characters pose a variety of problems, especially when records are imported from external sources that may use different modes of representing diacritical characters, such as the letters é and ó in Péter Jacsó. In some records such characters may be represented by their ASCII code, in other by the ANSI code, and in yet others by a combination of two characters. In some of the figure screen shots of Reference Manager these diacritical marks were not imported correctly. (See figure 7-4 with Jacsó spelled Jacs≤ and throughout Appendix B.) They are easy to correct but were left in the examples for illustration.

More complex is the situation in which characters must be used that are not available in the ANSI and extended ASCII characters, such as

Ł in Polish. When such letters are the lead characters in a personal, corporate, or geographic name, they can play havoc with sorting.

Windows itself has some control over sorting special characters. In the Windows Control Panel users can specify the language whose alphabetic filing rule is to be observed. The setting will control sorting in every application, not only in the bibliographic database. In EndNote the control may be overridden using the Sort Library command, but it may not be the perfect solution. ProCite also offers this option or the option to use only the base character for sorting. Micro-CDS/ISIS has the most flexible alternative: The designer can specify in a file the sort order of the special characters.

Ignoring Lead Terms in Sorting

Ignoring certain lead terms in the filing process is essential to file a title such as "The Magic of Correct Sorting" under the letter *M*. Some programs do this automatically. EndNote, for example, automatically ignores *A, An,* and *The* as lead terms. In a few programs the designer can specify the terms that are to be ignored in sorting (but those terms are shown in the display and when the records are printed). DB/TextWorks has a file for such lead terms that acts as a special kind of stop-word list for sorting only. Of course, users may simply omit the leading article or put it at the end of the title, for example, "Magic of Correct Sorting" or "Magic of Correct Sorting, The." Neither is a professional solution.

Designating nonfiling characters is fairly easy as long as only English-language materials are used. As soon as foreign-language materials are involved, the sorting limitations of the software become more obvious. With a Spanish-language collection, it is obvious that the definite articles *El, La, Los,* and *Las* should be among the nonfiling characters. However, there are exceptions, for example, the title "Las Vegas Gamble" certainly should not be filed under *V,* and the title "Los Angeles Burning" should be filed under *L* rather than *A*.

ProCite has a very smart solution for some of the filing problems: It has a generic stop list that applies to the title, keyword, and corporate author field and an author stop list that applies to personal names. Both can be easily modified on the fly by the user and even overridden temporarily. For the preceding examples, even if *Las* and *Los* are on the generic stop list, the user may enter a so-called hard space (by pressing the control, shift, and space keys simultaneously) after *Las* and *Los* that makes the program ignore the stop words for that record when sorting. The other option helps file personal names correctly, especially Arabic, Spanish, Italian, German, and Dutch names that have particles. For example, if "al-Razzaq, Abdul Faik" should be sorted under *R*, then including *al* in the author stop list would ignore *al* for sorting purposes. Of course, this still would be a problem for "Al, John"—an American author.

The point is that filing rules for lead terms need to be defined at the record level rather than the database level if there are foreign-language materials involved. Most of the software packages offered for public access cataloging can handle such situations in an elegant way that was invented almost forty years ago. One of the primary purposes of the indicators in the MARC records is the use of a filing indicator that instructs the program to ignore the first *n* characters of a title or a corporate name in sorting. It is a little tedious to enter this information for every record for which filing information must be specified, but it is an unambiguous way of doing it. Micro-CDS/ISIS offers an alternative by putting the nonfiling character string between triangular brackets in the records concerned. For example, the title, "<The >Cost of Living in Hawaii" will be filed under *C* but will still be printed with the definite article and without the brackets. This is the solution that could also be used to ignore special symbols at the beginning of a title. However, none of these solutions help when a number should be sorted as its alphabetic (spelled-out) equivalent.

Substitute String for Sorting

Another sort feature, offered only by Micro-CDS/ISIS, is the one that could be billed as the "101 Dalmatians" sort. Depending on the prevailing cataloging rules used by a library, this title should be sorted under *O* as if it were spelled out as "One Hundred and One Dalmatians." In Micro-CDS/ISIS this title is entered as "<101=One Hundred and One> Dalmatians," is filed indeed under the letter *O*, and is displayed as "101 Dalmatians."

10

Display, Print, and Download Functions

The last stages in the information retrieval process in terms of computer assistance are the displaying, printing, and/or downloading of the results. Many software packages take a simplified attitude to this phase by merely offering two or three predefined formats without any layout control for the designer, let alone the end user. Some programs provide tools for elaborate control of the content and layout of the output, and some software packages offer a variety of bibliographic formats out of the box, making easy the life of authors who publish in scholarly journals, each of which has its own specific citation styles.

Predefined and User-Definable Output Formats

Most software packages offer at least two predefined output formats: a short one for listing the results of a search and a long one for the full records. Many have no option for letting the users specify what data elements should be included in an output format. This is not a good approach because users often may need a format that is different from either of the predefined formats. Occasionally, users may want to have a quick format of their own that includes only the article title and the journal name; or only the author affiliation, the article title, and the publication year; or the title proper, the ISSN, and the publisher in the case of a serials directory.

Content Definition

Defining the data element content of the output (both of the short results list and the full output) should be as easy as picking data elements from a list, and doing so on the spur of the moment. Surprisingly few programs allow this option, even though it is commonly found in databases commercially published by DIALOG, Ovid, and SilverPlatter—at least for the full output. Even fewer are those microcomputer programs that offer users any control over the format of the short results list. As shown in figure 10-1, EndNote's built-in result list is a well-designed format providing good balance among the data elements shown. The content of the fields is obvious even without header labels. In ProCite the header labels serve well for instant re-sorting of the results list. (See figure 10-2.) Neither EndNote nor ProCite allows the user to change the content of this list. Reference Manager offers the most flexible and liberal solution by letting the user decide which data elements should be displayed in the short result list. (See figures 10-3 through 10-5.)

Figure 10-1   Results List Format in EndNote

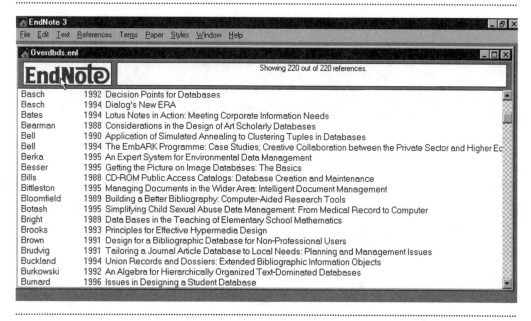

Figure 10-2   Results List Format in ProCite

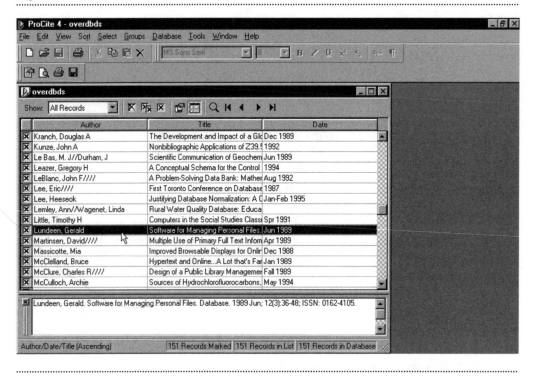

Figure 10-3   Results List Format in Reference Manager

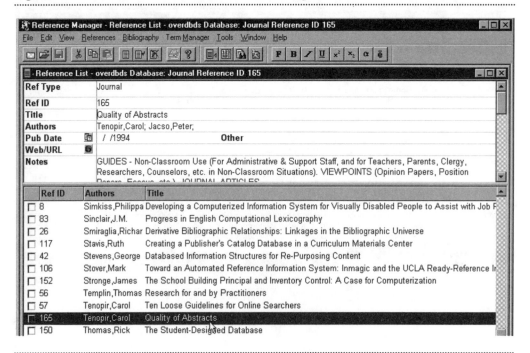

Figure 10-4   Customizing the Results List Content in Reference Manager

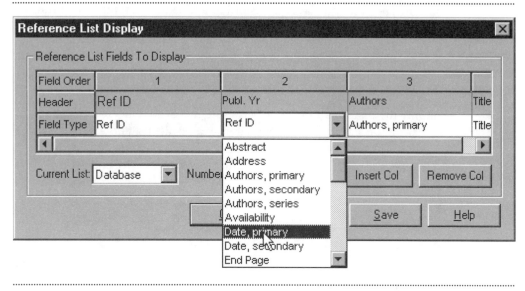

Figure 10-5   Revised Results List Format in Reference Manager

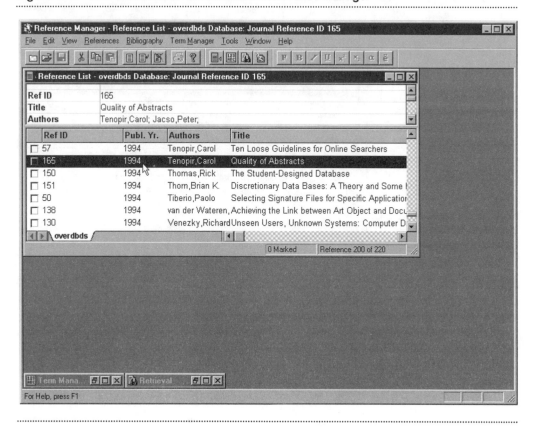

DB/TextWorks and Micro-CS/ISIS don't have a special results-list format. The latter displays one record at a time in whatever format the designer defined or the user chose.

ProCite has an excellent option that is not strictly a results-list format, but a highly efficient alternative to decide if an item should be included in the full output list or not. It also offers the fastest and simplest way of browsing, searching, and displaying the results. In figure 10-6, only the display and print aspects of QuickSearch are shown. The right part of the screen can be split between a results list and a record display pane. The user has an impressive level of control in customizing both the results-list pane and the record pane. (See figures 10-7 and 10-8.)

Figure 10-6   ProCite's Results Preview Format

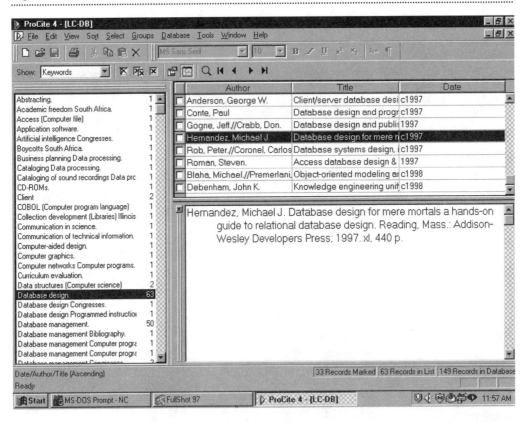

Figure 10-7   Customizing the Content of the Results List Pane in ProCite

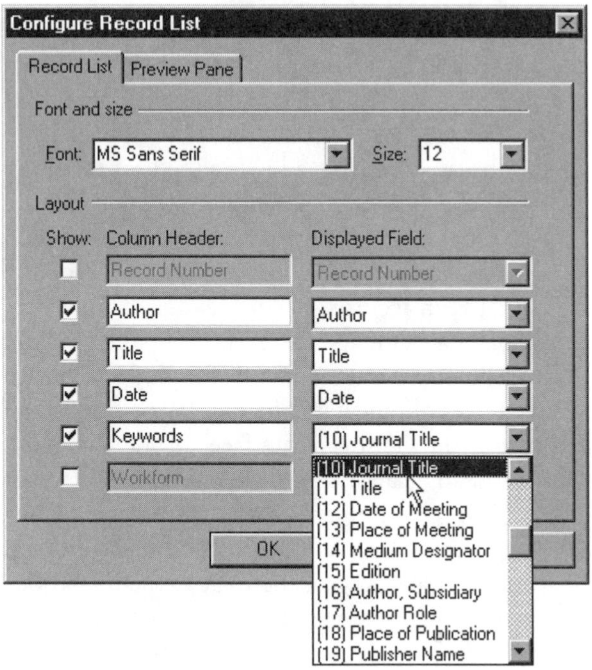

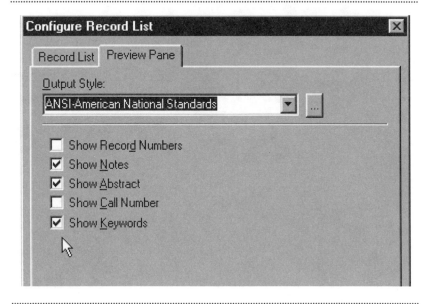

Figure 10-8   Customizing the Content and Style of the Record Pane in ProCite

Layout Definition

Designing and defining the layout of the output is a more complicated process than content definition. It is not really appropriate to improvise the layout. Several programs offer powerful options for layout control that are best decided upon in the database design and development phase rather than allowing the user to choose from various layouts.

Layout features pertain to both the layout of the pages and the individual records. Page layout includes the definition of the margins, printing of headers and footers, use and indention of headings, and spacing between records. Record layout includes horizontal and vertical spacing of data elements within records, font type and font size, punctuation and labeling of data elements, and special treatment of first and last occurrences of repeatable fields.

The graphical interfaces of the Windows and Mac operating systems and applications make layout design a far easier task than in the DOS and UNIX environments. Dragging and dropping data elements on a form that mimics the size of the screen or the print page help optimize the grouping and positioning of the data elements. So do the dynamic stretching and pushing of the margin lines that show the changing lineup of the fields as the area for displaying and printing increases and decreases. This is the approach of DB/TextWorks or Microsoft Access. The bibliography formatting and management software also offer graphical help in defining the page layout. Figures 10-9 through 10-11 show the layout specification controls for DB/TextWorks, ProCite, and Reference Manager.

Figure 10-9   Page Layout Design in DB/TextWorks

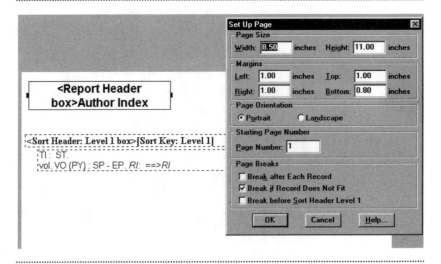

Figure 10-10 Page Layout Design in ProCite

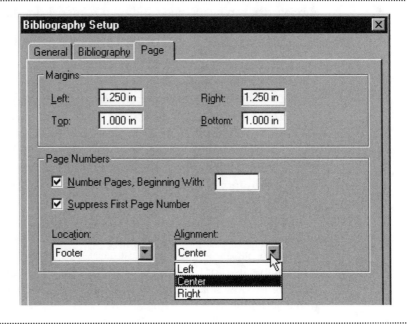

Figure 10-11 Page Layout Design in Reference Manager

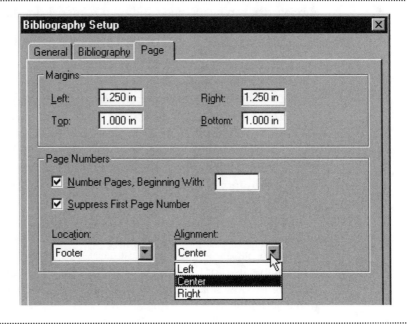

Most of the programs offer the preview of actual records in a separate window. The designer may see the impact of making a narrower margin, of moving a data element from one position to the other, or of changing the font style and font size from 12 point Courier to 11 point Arial. This instant feedback with real data provides the opportunity to experiment with the best layout using a variety of records with different content and length.

Widow and Orphan Control

A widow is a short paragraph line (or part of a record) at the beginning of a page. An orphan is a stranded single line (or part of a record) at the bottom of a page. Widow and orphan control are atypical capabilities of Micro-CDS/ISIS that allow the designer to specify that a new record should be moved to the next page if there are fewer than a given number of lines left on the page. This can avoid splitting records across pages. In the case of a very large bibliography, this may not work out perfectly, but downloading the result list and then chiseling it using a word processor is always an option. For example, if only a word or two flow over to the next page, reducing the font size from 12 to 11 for the abstract could solve the problem. The readers would not be appalled, if they noticed it at all.

Designing the layout at the record level is a more complex task. All of the bibliography management programs offer a large number of citation formats that can be modified and used as models for the specification of a new record layout. It is like improving a frozen pizza picked up at the supermarket by adding some extra cheese, a drop of olive oil, and a tad of basil before putting it in the microwave, which is much easier than starting out with just the dough. The wide variety of predefined citation formats in all of the bibliography management software may make it unnecessary to ever use the layout and content design options in these programs. Figure 10-12 shows how a citation format can be customized in Reference Manager. For example, the designer may select the font style and size and may choose from a large number of output style formats such as two versions of the Turabian format, the American Sociological Association's style, or the American Psychological Association's style.

Graphical wizardry is not very helpful when inserting punctuation marks between data elements, dealing with repeatable occurrences of fields, and handling special situations of the first and last occurrences of a repeatable field or the absence of a field. Previewing the records before printing or downloading them will help the designer see where additional adjustments must be made on a record-by-record basis.

Figure 10-12   Customizing a Predefined Citation Format in Reference Manager

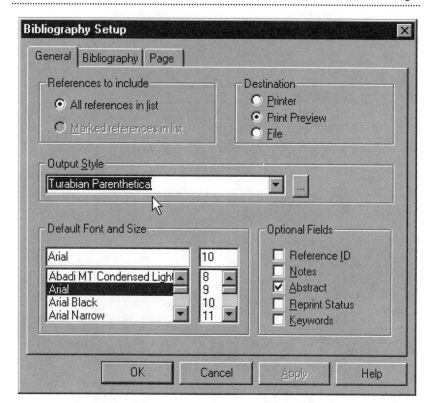

As for content customization, the designer may change the punctuation between data elements, the labels that precede the field values, or insert line feeds between data elements as illustrated in figure 10-13.

With Micro-CDS/ISIS and DB/TextWorks designers are left much more on their own (unless they buy the Library Guide sample database for DB/TextWorks that may take care of all the database definition, worksheet, and output design issues). Record layout design is a text-coding activity, but DB/TextWorks prompts the designer to provide conditional or unconditional strings before or after the field and to display a text if the field has no value, such as *s.l.* if the place of publication field is not known or was left empty.

Printing some sample records is the proof of the pudding, especially as the screen's mimicking of the printed output may not be perfect. For example, in spite of its superior preview capabilities, DB/TextWorks does

Figure 10-13   Customizing a Predefined Citation Content in Reference Manager

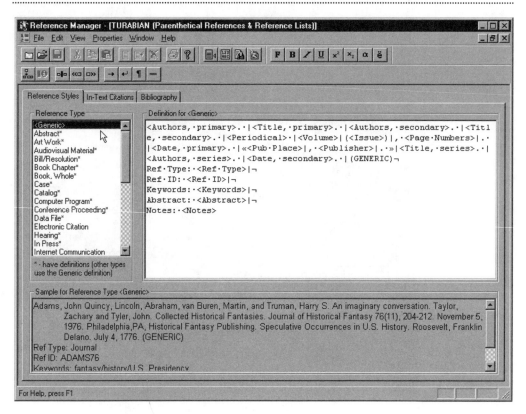

not properly indicate the vertical spacing between records. Micro-CDS/ISIS may have the most powerful output formatting options of all the sample programs, but output formatting is a task that not even the nicely designed Windows version can help with. It remains a rather cryptic and involved task along with the sort specifications.

Export Formats

Most of the programs offer some options for exporting the data either in the proprietary format of some widely used other bibliographic programs or in a standard exchange format such as comma-and-quote-delimited format or tab-delimited format. Only Micro-CDS/ISIS offers the exporting of records in MARC Communications format. DB/TextWorks' only export format is its own tagged format, unless the MARC import/export utility developed by MITINET is purchased at around $250—a steep price for this bidirectional conversion software.

The reluctance of the software producers to provide a variety of export formats is somewhat understandable because they don't want to make it too easy for users to take their data and migrate it to another program that can import records in such formats. Of course, the software packages that have sophisticated print facilities can be programmed to create a tab-delimited or a comma-and-quote-delimited output format, but the MARC Communications format is beyond the scope of the print formatting facilities.

One relatively new output requirement is the ability to produce records in HTML format that, in turn, can be uploaded to a Web page. This capability is just evolving at this time, but it is something that potential users look forward to. Even if there is no direct HTML capability available in textual database management software, there are ways of creating the output as an HTML file. First, the output can be downloaded in plain-text format (possibly losing some of the formatting) and then imported into a word processing program that in turn can create a fair HTML version. Also, shareware and freeware programs can convert text files and files in other standard file formats into HTML format. Many of the new Web authoring software programs also import standard file formats—among others—from textual database management software. This is the first step for the simplest kind of Web publishing of textual data that is an evolving technology (and the subject of another book).

Interface Considerations

The interface of the software represents the bridge between the users and the components of the software such as the data entry, retrieval, and sort modules. The interface is like the office receptionist who welcomes the customers, recognizes their needs, and provides direct answers or directs them to the specialists.

The interface forms the user's first impression about the software and the database; therefore, its role is critical. It should be accommodating for first-time visitors and succinct for returning ones if they so wish. Judging an interface is rather subjective. Much depends on the user's preferences and prior experience. What may be pleasing for a total novice is not necessarily appropriate for the user who just wants to get down to brass tacks quickly and do a fast search.

Interface Types and Levels

There are three major interface types: command-driven, menu-driven, and template-driven. At different stages of the retrieval transaction, the software may deploy any of these interface types. For example, users may see a template for entering the search terms in the appropriate cells to specify a word in the title and a date in the publication year. They may then be presented with a menu that offers options to display the results, sort them, or print them. When the sort option is selected, a template may again be displayed. From the template, users can select the primary and secondary fields for sorting from the list of sortable fields. They may also set their preference for filing the results by dictionary rules (where lower- and uppercase characters are indifferent) or by code values used by the computer to represent data (where all the terms starting with an uppercase character will precede the terms starting with the same letter in lowercase format). These options are often presented with check boxes and radio buttons. Check boxes indicate several simultaneous choices; radio buttons indicate an exclusive choice. Check boxes are used, for example, to select the fields that should be included in the output. Radio buttons are used with options that are mutually exclusive, such as filing preferences. At the downloading stage the user may need to provide a command, such as specifying the destination drive and the name of the file.

To accommodate users with different backgrounds, the software should offer at least two different interface levels: one for the beginner user and another for the advanced users. Choosing the level may be determined as much by the actual information request as by the experience of the user. Even an advanced user may prefer the simple-search template when only a quick search is needed for a known item, for example, when the user knows the author, title, and publication year. Templates or menus for complex searches should also be available so, for example, the user can look for specific document types in specific languages published in specific years on a subject. The interface should present a template for the advanced interface with check boxes to mark the language and document type preferences or should offer choices one by one to limit the subject search by document type, language, and publication year in consecutive steps.

From the database designers' points of view, the software should allow them to customize the interfaces to the application, in terms of both content and layout. Surprisingly few software packages provide the designer the freedom of choice to create search templates that match the best characteristics of the database.

Ergonomics

Even the software capable of producing the best databases can be of little use if the interface is not ergonomically well-designed. This is probably the most subjective aspect of evaluating software. However, there are some de facto standards that are commonly followed by designers and have been reinforced by the widespread use of graphical software environment such as Windows and the Mac OS.

Of course, it is not enough merely to have fancy graphic symbols on the screen instead of text. Sometimes plain text can be more effective than an obscure icon to identify an option; a button labeled "print" is more effective than a hazy symbol of a printer. Both Apple and Microsoft issued formal guidelines for designing interfaces, and more and more mainstream applications follow those guidelines. However, all software need not look identical in presenting options, but basic rules should be observed. For example, selecting multiple items from a pull- or roll-down menu of journal names in an abstracting/indexing database should be allowed by using the control key and the left mouse button. Selecting a continuous range of these entries should be possible by clicking on the first item, then scrolling down to the last item desired and pressing the shift key.

If some functions are not applicable at certain stages of the search process, they should be indicated by graying out the disabled functions. For example, the print button should be grayed out until the user marks at least one record for printing. Selected items should be clearly identified with an X in the check box next to the item or with a check mark.

Intuitiveness is the key to good ergonomic design. The interface is intuitive if the majority of users can guess how to navigate through the steps, initiate an action, go back to the previous screen, or change the database—without having to look up the process in the help file. Interface design can help a lot in keeping the user interested and gratified. However, some features can be communicated to users only through text. Then the documentation and the help files come into play.

Documentation and Help Facilities

Common experience shows that users don't read the printed documentation even if it is readily available at the computer. Often, the printed documentation for the database is misplaced or gets buried under other materials in the carrel or on the desk near the computers.

An essential feature of good software in that it offers informative and effective help to users who need directions but are reluctant to ask anyone for assistance. Well-structured and deeply indexed help files are common practice in the late 1990s. These help files are browsable through a table of contents page and searchable by keywords that indicate which sections in the online help file discuss the topic and take the user there. The more sophisticated software packages provide context-sensitive help information. When the user clicks on the help button, the program recognizes the context from which the user asks for help and displays the section of the help file that discusses the topic. For example, when a user is at the printing phase but does not know how to mark items to be printed, context-sensitive software would show the sections about selecting print formats, selecting items to be printed, and defining print destinations. The user could then click on the section about selecting items to be printed for further information.

Database developers, on the other hand, are willing to use well-written software documentation, and they indeed need to have printed guides and to read the manual for nitty-gritty details. It is no accident that one of the most often cited programs discussed in this book, DB/TextWorks, also stands out in terms of its documentation. It provides in-depth information about all the features of the software, and it is well structured, superbly illustrated, and thoroughly indexed. The text is also available as a help file to use when the manual is not at the developer's fingertips.

Database developers should be able to provide their own help files with the specifics of the data content itself and with examples that refer to the actual database. With the advent of remotely searched databases, such online help becomes even more important, as there is no other way to provide guidance for the users who log in from the other end of the world in the wee hours. The information should be readily available and easily accessible and should discuss the content of the database and the software features. Although animated and annotated screen shots that illustrate a process are very effective, they are available only for the mainstream programs that sell in the millions, like Microsoft Word. Perhaps with the increasing popularity of remote access, publishers of other software packages will also find it beneficial to provide how-to illustrations for the users who are not inclined to read screens of text just to learn how to download records after a search.

A final word: This book has offered guidance to help you build a good database in terms of content and software. Content criteria remain relatively stable. Software criteria keep evolving as many talented programmers make their work available on the Web. Before you build your database, build your checklist of the criteria that are most important to you. Then get the demonstration versions of some of the most promising programs and put them through their paces before you set out to design your database content and structure.

APPENDIX A
URLs for Software Products

AskSAM	http://www.asksam.com
BookWhere 2000	http://www.bookwhere.com
Data Magician	http://www.folland.com
DB/TextWorks	http://www.inmagic.com
EndNote	http://www.niles.com
Fangorn	http://www.bib.wau.nl
FileMaker Pro	http://www.filemaker.com
Library Master	http://www.balboa-software.com
MARC Review	http://www.tlcdelivers.com/tlc/ marcrevw.htm
MARC RTP	http://willow.canberra.edu.au/~jlt/ marc.html
MARC Transformer	http://www.mitinet.com
Micro-CDS/ISIS of UNESCO	http://www.unesco.org
Microsoft Access	http://www.microsoft.com
MITINET Transform	http://www.mitinet.com
ProCite	http://www.risinc.com
Reference Manager	http://www.risinc.com

APPENDIX B
Import and Export Formats
of Bibliographic Records

Programs identify the beginnings and ends of records, fields, and subfields in their own peculiar ways by using special symbols, punctuation,
field tags, and subfield codes. As long as you work with a single program
you may not even be aware of these peculiarities. However, when you
have to import records from someone else's database or send your data to
someone who uses a different textual database management program,
you or your partner may need to learn the import and export formats of
the sending and receiving programs. The following examples show the
same record in import and export formats used by the sample programs
discussed in the book. Special and accented characters in records downloaded from mainframe computers may appear as weird symbols on a PC
or Mac. These were left in the examples for illustration, but they need to
be corrected in real-life situations.

Tagged Format of EndNote

EndNote's tagged format identifies the fields with the percent (%) sign
and a letter.

```
%0 Book
%A Jacs≤, P⊛ter
%D 1992
%T CD-ROM software, dataware, and hardware : evaluation, selection, and installa
tion
%B Database searching series ; no. 4
%C Englewood, Colo.
%I Libraries Unlimited
%P xv, 256
%@ 0872879070
%L Z681.3.o67 j33 1991
025.3/0285
%K Optical disks.
Libraries Automation.
CD-ROMs.
%0 91030705 //r952
P⊛ter Jacs≤.
Includes bibliographical references and index.
```

Comma-and-Quote Delimited Format of EndNote

The comma-and-quote delimited format is the most common import/export format that is also used by spreadsheet and mainstream database management programs. All data elements are separated by commas and are preceded and followed by single quotation marks (' '). If a field does not appear in a record, the double quote and comma (" ",) string still appears as a space holder.

```
"A","","Jacs≤, P@ter","","","CD-ROM software, dataware, and hardware : evaluatio
n, selection, and installation","","","","","","","","","","","","","","Englewoo
d, Colo.","Libraries Unlimited","1992","","","","","","","","","","","","",""
,"","","","","","","0872879070","91030705 //r952
P@ter Jacs≤.
Includes bibliographical references and index.","","","Optical disks.
Libraries Automation.
CD-ROMs."
```

Reference Manager Format

Reference Manager identifies the field with a field tag followed by two spaces, a hyphen, and a space. The record end is indicated by the ER - string.

```
TY  - BOOK
AU  - Jacs≤, P.
PY  - 1992
BT  - CD-ROM software, dataware, and hardware : evaluation, selection, and insta
llation
CY  - Englewood, Colo.
PB  - Libraries Unlimited
SP  - xv, 256
KW  - Optical disks.
Libraries Automation.
CD-ROMs.
ER  -
```

DB/TextWorks Comma-and-Quote Delimited Format

The comma-and-quote delimited format of the DB/TextWorks sample is similar to that shown for EndNote. However, the double quotes are not used as space holders. The other differences are because the record definition of the two programs is different. The fields used are different, and so is the order of the fields. However, the syntax is identical.

```
,,,,"CD-ROM software, dataware, and hardware","evaluation, selection, and instal
lation","Jacs≤, P@ter.",,"P@ter Jacs≤.",,,,"Englewood, Colo.","Libraries Unlimite
d","1992","xv, 256 p. ill. 28 cm.",,"Database searching series","Optical disks.|
Libraries -- Automation.|CD-ROMs.",,,"0872879070",,,,,,,,,,,,,,,,,,,,,,,,,,,,,,,,,,
,,,,"   91030705 //r952","3/24/98"
```

DB/TextWorks Labeled Format

DB/TextWorks labeled format precedes the field value that is separated by a space from the label. If the label is a compound term (that is, includes a space), it is enclosed between apostrophes ('). The end of the record is identified by a single dollar sign ($) that stands alone on a line.

```
Title CD-ROM software, dataware, and hardware
Subtitle evaluation, selection, and installation
Author Jacs≤, P@ter.
Responsibility P@ter Jacs≤.
Place Englewood, Colo.
Publisher Libraries Unlimited
'Pub Date' 1992
'Physical Description' xv, 256 p. ill. 28 cm.
Series Database searching series
Descriptors Optical disks.
; Libraries -- Automation.
; CD-ROMs.
ISBN 0872879070
'LC Card'    91030705 //r952
$
```

WinISIS Tagged Format

The WinISIS tagged format uses the superscript caret (^) subfield delimiter and the alphabetical subfield codes to identify the subfields such as ^a for the place of publication, ^b for the name of the publisher, and ^c for the copyright year. The copyright year is recorded as c1992. This is the reason for the ^cc1992. Technically, the © copyright symbol should have been used, but because of former character symbol limits of the operating system, the display, and printers in earlier years, the letter *c* was accepted as the copyright symbol in the imprint field.

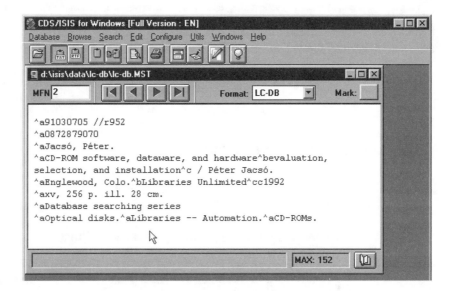

WinISIS ISO Export Format

In the WinISIS ISO export format, the data elements are preceded by a record directory. (The field separator is &; the record separator is #.) This stream of characters has a structure that remains hidden for the untrained person. The first 24 positions make up the leader part of the record. The first five positions of the leader indicate the length of the records in characters. For example, our sample record is 448 characters long. The leader is followed from position 25 of the record, known as the *directory*. It defines for each data element the tag and length of each field and their relative position from the first field in the record. These values are automatically calculated by the export program, not by humans. The accented characters were not converted appropriately, but the WinISIS import/export utility allows the designer to define how to translate accented characters.

```
0044800000000014500045000100018000000200013000181000016000312450100000472 6000470
0147300000250019449900028002196900017002476900002700264690001100291&^a91030705 //r9
52&^a0872879070&^aJacsó, Péter.&^aCD-ROM software, dataware, and hardware^bevalu
ation, selection, and installation^c / Péter Jacsó.&^aEnglewood, Colo.^bLibrarie
s Unlimited^cc1992&^axv, 256 p. ill. 28 cm.&^aDatabase searching series&^aOptica
l disks.&^aLibraries -- Automation.&^aCD-ROMs.&#
```

MARC Communications Format

The MARC Communications format is very similar to the ISO format, being an implementation of the standard format for exchanging bibliographic information as defined by the International Standards Organization known as ISO 2709. The same similarity applies also to the inappropriate translation of the accented characters discussed in the previous example. Again, these record formats are generated and interpreted by the programs; humans have to look at them only if the import/export operation was not successful so they can spot the possible reason for the problem.

```
00792cam  2200241 a 450000100190000000030004000190050017000230080041000400100002300
0527020000250008104000180010605000250012408200190014910000200016824501050018826000
05200293300003300345440003900378504005100417650001900468650002700487650001300514
▲    91030705 //r952▲DLC▲19950213081810.1▲910807s1992    coua      b    001 0 eng
 ▲   ▼a0872879070 :▼c$35.00▲  ▼aDLC▼cDLC▼dDLC▲00▼aZ681.3.O67▼bJ33 1991▲00▼a025.3/
0285▼220▲10▼aJacsΓo, PΓeter.▲10▼aCD-ROM software, dataware, and hardware :▼beval
uation, selection, and installation /▼cPΓeter JacsΓo.▲0 ▼aEnglewood, Colo. :▼bLi
braries Unlimited,▼c1992.▲  ▼axv, 256 p. :▼bill. ;▼c28 cm.▲ 0▼aDatabase searchin
g series ;▼vno. 4▲  ▼aIncludes bibliographical references and index.▲ 0▼aOptical
 disks.▲ 0▼aLibraries▼xAutomation.▲ 0▼aCD-ROMs.▲  ▼a    91030705 //r952▲↵
```

Index

Note: Because the entire book is about databases, the term "database" is not used as an entry point in this index.

Péter Jacsó is an associate professor in the Department of Information and Computer Sciences' Library and Information Science Program at the University of Hawaii. He has been developing textual databases for libraries and information centers and has been teaching database design courses for more than twenty years. Jacsó won the 1998 ALISE/Pratt-Severn Faculty Innovation Award for his course development work related to database design, implementation, and publishing. He has published extensively in scholarly and trade journals of library and information science and technology and has been a consultant for various U.N. agencies and major online and CD-ROM database publishers. Jacsó is a columnist for *Computers in Libraries, Database,* and *Information Today* and has won several awards for his writings, including the 1998 Louis Shores/Oryx Press Award for his discerning database reviews.

F. Wilfrid Lancaster is Professor Emeritus in the Graduate School of Library and Information Science at the University of Illinois where he has taught courses relating to information transfer, bibliometrics, bibliographic organization, and the evaluation of library and information services. He continues to serve as editor of *Library Trends.* Lancaster was appointed University Scholar for 1989–1992. He is the author of eleven books, six of which have received national awards, and has three times received Fulbright fellowships for research and teaching abroad. From the American Society for Information Science he has received both the Award of Merit and the Outstanding Information Science Teacher award. Lancaster has been involved in a wide range of consulting activities, including service for UNESCO and other agencies of the United Nations. He is coauthor of the 1997 book *Technology and Management in Library and Information Services* and is writing a book on the potential applications of artificial intelligence and expert system technologies within libraries.